FOR GOD&
COUNTRY

A DISCUSSION ON
SERVANT LEADERSHIP

Steve,
Thank you for the
love and support as I seek
to glorify God. I am so thankful
for your brotherhood and mentorship.
I love you guys and I'm
for you as you serve
Him.

In Christ,

Col 3:17

FOREWORD BY DR. CHRISTOPHER SHANNON

MIKE ROOT

LUCIDBOOKS

For God and Country
A Discussion on Servant Leadership

Copyright © 2019 by Mike Root

Published by Lucid Books in Houston, TX
www.LucidBooksPublishing.com

ISBN-10: 1-63296-325-6
ISBN-13: 978-1-63296-325-3
eISBN-10: 1-63296-338-8
eISBN-13: 978-1-63296-338-3

Unless otherwise indicated, Scripture quotations are taken from the ESV® Bible (The Holy Bible, English Standard Version®), copyright © 2001 by Crossway, a publishing ministry of Good News Publishers. Used by permission. All rights reserved.

Scripture quotations marked (NIV) are taken from the Holy Bible, New International Version®, NIV®. Copyright ©1973, 1978, 1984, 2011 by Biblica, Inc.™ Used by permission of Zondervan. All rights reserved worldwide. www.zondervan.com The "NIV" and "New International Version" are trademarks registered in the United States Patent and Trademark Office by Biblica, Inc.™

Scripture quotations marked (KJV) are taken from the King James Version (KJV): King James Version, public domain.

Special Sales: Most Lucid Books titles are available in special quantity discounts. Custom imprinting or excerpting can also be done to fit special needs. Contact Lucid Books at Info@LucidBooksPublishing.com.

Soli Deo Gloria

Table of Contents

Special Thanks

To my wife, who shows me what grace and true selfless sacrificial love look like.

To my mom, who has given me the greatest example of the love of Christ toward others.

To my dad, who always challenges me to be the best at whatever endeavor I am seeking next.

To my nana and papa, who have shown me what living for Christ means.

To my stepfather, who has shown me what the kindness and patience of Christ are.

And to my little brother, to whom I try to set the greatest example.

Foreword

"For even the Son of Man did not come to be served, but to serve" (Mark 10:45 NIV). Christ's command for leaders to first serve their followers seems simple; however, this call comes with challenges which can take on various levels of complexity often reinforced by specific workplace policies and procedures. Christ's encounters as a leader included many complex challenges related to the embedded cultural norms, policies, and laws of His time. While Christ was explicit about the importance of adhering to governing laws, He stood in stark contrast to the cultural norm that demanded loyal service by the follower to the leader. He demonstrated the importance of the leader serving their followers first. It is this and other Christ-like service examples that are the underpinnings for the roadmap Mike outlines in his book. The roadmap includes insightful, inspiring, and inviting words and stories about how to lead effectively, regardless of the complexities associated with serving God and serving our country in the dynamics of the government workplace.

Having been a veteran in service to God, a leadership development course instructor for over 14 years, and someone with more than three decades of service in the federal government, I can testify to the inspirational power, validity, and relevance of this book. It was as his commanding officer in the Air Force Reserve Officer Training Course (AFROTC) detachment that I first met Mike Root. Over the past nine years, I have witnessed his growth from a cadet to the stellar Air Force officer he is today. During his time at AFROTC, I was reasonably sure he knew of God. However, at that time I did not ask Him directly about his walk with Christ. I tried to demonstrate my love for God through my daily walk before Him, the detachment cadets, and my staff without crossing the delicate boundaries associated with leading in a government workplace. I fashioned my leadership philosophy around the servant guidance example Christ provided during His walk with His disciples and interactions with others. Even so, my purposeful leadership demonstration did not include direct engagement about their specific walk with Christ. My restrained spiritual zeal was my attempt at executing my responsibilities as a military leader to govern the practice and perception of religious proselytizing. It is this challenging friction of leading and following in the government workplace while serving God that Mike addresses in his book.

Mike's words and stories often transported me to memorable moments that included life-altering spiritual experiences. Most of my retrospection was about days of me sitting in the church pews listening to preachers and others share the Word of God, often moving me to think/verbalize phrases of confirmation like "Amen!," "Preach, Preacher!," and "Say that, Pastor!" These words of casual affirmations and acknowledgments were often a part of the tenor in some congregations where I attended church, meant to encourage the preacher or speaker and acknowledge that the words being shared truly resonated with a specific follower. Mike's compassionate request to the servants of God to renew their call to "go" and share the gospel has prompted this level of emotional and thought-provoking response from me.

I am thankful for Mike's willingness to share the Word of God in an encouraging yet matter-of-fact tone. His straightforward use of words reminded me, positively, that the "word of God is . . . sharper than any twoedged sword . . . and is a discerner of the thoughts and intents of the heart" (Heb. 4:12 KJV). The sincerity and directness of his writing ensures that this book does not fall prey to the pronouncement in 2 Timothy 4:3, which asserts that people will summon teachers who will not teach sound doctrine; instead, the teachers will focus on suiting the desires of the followers. Mike has shaped a doctrinally based message that will inspire the believer to action. He bolsters this call to action with insights about the need for the leader to garner a keen sense of awareness for the challenges of sharing the love of Christ while serving in the government workplace.

Sharing the love of Christ in the workplace requires leaders, chiefly followers of Christ in a leadership role, to grapple with how they will execute Christ's call to "go" in a somewhat religion intolerant, policy-driven workplace. While government workplace policies do not openly forbid religious discussions, the policies' inferences seem to discourage such spiritual dialogues. It is this dichotomy between serving Christ and serving as leaders in a government workplace that drew me even deeper into Mike's book to learn more about how to mitigate some of these challenges.

Mike outlines some fundamental biblical principles for why we must emulate Christ's servant leadership example to help us navigate the complexities of the intersection of living for God and serving our country. This Christ-like example focuses on demonstrating our love for our followers. Mike acknowledges that the challenges of executing this type of love can be perplexing, considering the policies and underlying culture of the government workplace. Mitigating these challenges will require we have a firm spiritual foundation. Mike highlights three of the critical elements needed to ensure we are standing on a firm foundation. These components include the need for the indwelling of the Spirit, accompanied by a strong relationship with Christ and bolstered by a deep connection with the Word and the need for a consistent prayer life. Even with a firm foundation, it is essential to understand that the challenges will not shrink; in fact, the intensity of the spiritual challenges will most likely increase. The inference is that our workplace is part of our spiritual battlefield. This spiritual battlefield requires us to adorn the proper warrior attire.

The Bible describes the proper warrior attire as the whole armor of God. Mike coaches the reader through the importance of each piece of the armor of God. He also warns that all parts are critical to victory on the battlefield. Even though the words *armor*, *warrior*, and *battlefield* can invoke thoughts of aggressive confrontations, the Bible proclaims the need for believers to battle gracefully. Scripture directs that we share the gospel in a non-quarrelsome and gentle way. Properly developed and nurtured workplace relationships can be catalysts for sharing Christ in such a dynamic environment. For the leader and follower who want to build these types of relationships that will pave the way for the opportunities to share Christ, this book is your inroad to shaping such a dynamic environment.

Mike shares his first-person perspective of the challenges associated with serving God and serving one's country in the dynamics of the government workplace. As a member of the military and an individual who has declared his devotion and love for Jesus Christ, he is qualified to champion this dialogue. Mike submits that navigating this intersection between the critical nodes of service to God and country is not without its trials. Nevertheless, he reminds us that the dynamic environment is navigable when properly understood and when we appropriately employ biblically based principles.

Your encounter with the contents of this book will beckon a positive response for you to take action to rejuvenate your commitment to sharing your love for Christ. I found Mike's careful analysis of the challenges associated with sharing one's faith in the workplace, his personal experiences in this endeavor, and his biblically based coaching to meet the challenges both educational and inspiring. Bottom line, if the intersection of living for God and serving your country has and continues to prove problematic for you, then I encourage you to read this book with an open heart and mind. Read it from cover to cover, then re-read it multiple times, and then hold on to it as a reference for how to effectively live for Christ in what can be one of the Christian's primary mission fields, our workplaces.

Dr. Christopher Shannon is an Assistant Professor for Leadership and Ethics at Air University, eSchool for Graduate Professional Military Education in Montgomery, Alabama. He is a devoted servant of Christ, with over three decades as a federal government employee (military and civilian). He and his wife of 35 years reside in Troy, Alabama. They are the proud parents of three sons and grandparents of six grandkids.

Introduction

I'm sitting in a small room in the middle of Pakistan, serving my second tour overseas. As I consider my career in the military, I wonder if my brothers and sisters in arms, many of whom are also my brothers and sisters in Christ, have struggled with the idea of serving both God and country.

This tour is much different from my last. I'm in a remote location, far removed from modern comforts, yet I'm closer to God than ever before. I've been blessed with a season of spiritual growth, spurred by a sharpening of faith through seminary. Now, the Holy Spirit has laid on my heart a time of meditation on what it means to faithfully serve our mighty God while also serving our great country. The answer, though multifaceted, inevitably points to leadership.

You may wonder, "Why another book on leadership?" Simply put, after reading many books on leadership and many more on serving God, I've noticed a chasm between those two forms of service. But, I feel it's important to know what it means to serve God *and* country.

What does it look like to serve God *while* serving our country? More so, what does this service look like from a biblical perspective? This book will highlight what the Bible says about serving in any government or civil servant capacity, and it includes those who serve with me in the armed forces, elected officials, national park employees, and other government jobs such as in the United States Postal Service. In whatever facet you serve our country, this book is for you. If you work in the private sector, this book will help as you serve God in your workplace, though you may have fewer restrictions than those in government jobs. The beauty of the Bible is that it transcends occupation, title, rank, and any position of authority.

If you believe the Scriptures are the infallible, inerrant Word of God as I do, then you can believe there is a reason you are serving right where you are today. The difference between this book and many others is the focus on Bible principles. To help you apply Scripture to your service, I include helpful analogies and stories specifically for those of us serving our country in any capacity, though these principles extend to any vocation. My prayer is that you will join me as we seek to serve God faithfully, all the while serving our country as we are called to do. Whatever you are doing right this moment is exactly what God has planned for you to do, and you are exactly where He has placed you to serve. Serving Him with a loving and loyal heart and demonstrating and glorifying Christ in all we do is also serving our country faithfully. As we will see, there is purpose to our servanthood, both as followers of Christ and as servants to our country. How will you display Christ in your service?

Chapter 1

Servant Leadership

What is servant leadership? Is this seemingly paradoxical term even a real leadership style? How can we be expected to lead others while simultaneously serving them? If we look at these questions from a purely corporate perspective, we can come up with many different and quite appealing answers. There are countless books that rightly define what servant leadership *can* look like. But there is only one book that provides us a pure understanding of what true servant leadership *should* look like.

Have you ever enjoyed a job simply because you had a good boss? What made that individual stand out to you as a good leader? At some point, they probably demonstrated a legitimate caring attitude for you and your fellow employees, or at the very least displayed characteristics of someone who could be trusted. To be a leader, one must have followers and, in some form, influence. Good bosses or leaders are people who inspire others to easily follow them, even when the way ahead is not so easy. To inspire others to serve, leaders must be willing to serve those whom they lead. So what makes someone a so-called "servant leader"? Well, a servant leader is just that: a servant who just so happens to be leading others. As much as we like to coin new phrases and come up with

catchy titles, there is no need to dilute the meaning with
fancy words or scholarly titles. One of the best definitions of
a servant leader I've found comes from the book *The Servant
Leader,* which describes this type of leader as someone who
sees leadership as "an act of service."[1] When we recognize that
leadership is about serving those who work for us rather than
serving ourselves, then we have entered into the beginning
stages of servant leadership.

This definition of servant leadership is simple. The dif-
ficulty is knowing how to serve yet lead. To answer this, we
must look to the ultimate servant and leader: Jesus. Jesus displayed the epitome of servanthood and leadership, revealing
the perfect unity of these two ideas at work. While we can
point to many great leaders throughout history who have
effectively displayed each quality, only Jesus has taken servanthood to the point of death on a cross for our salvation,
and only Jesus has modeled leadership from the foundation of
the world to the throne in Heaven. Jesus is, and will ever be,
the only one who has given us the perfect example of servant
leadership. Though we cannot be a perfect servant leader, we
can find encouragement and comfort knowing that Christ
has already conquered this daunting task and left us with His
Spirit to help us and lead us in His name and for His glory.
Jesus is the line between secular and biblical leadership styles.

What's the Difference?

The hard line between secular leadership styles and biblical
servant leadership is the end result: One honors and glorifies
the leader or the company; the other honors and glorifies
Jesus Christ. Only in the Bible do we see the model for servant

1. Ken Blanchard and Phil Hodges, *The Servant Leader* (Nashville:
Thomas Nelson, 2003), 18.

leadership. To be clear, the service I speak of is first and foremost being a servant of Christ. It is then, and only then, that we can compassionately and wholeheartedly serve others. If at any point we serve only to gratify ourselves, then our service is not servant leadership but selfish leadership. No matter the good intentions we might have, if the focus of our service is not resting on Christ, then our subsequent leadership practices will be in vain. When we serve others selflessly, we bring glory to the name of Jesus and honor the example He has given us, living in obedience to His command and walking in His will for us. We were created to glorify and imitate Christ, for we were created in His image. The point of focus is where many leadership books differ. Most commonly, we're told to focus on ourselves or to make some characteristic changes that will better our leadership traits. Quite honestly, these things may very well make you a better "leader." However, if your chief goal in leadership is simply getting people to follow you, then I would ask you, who are *you* following?

Whether we like to admit it or not, we are all following, or at the very least emulating, someone significant in our lives. Many of us find ourselves enthralled in television or movie characters who depict what we wish life could be like. Maybe you follow someone on social media sites, someone who gives you glimpses of an ideal life through the selective exciting moments they post online. You may be following someone close to you, be it an actual leader or someone in a position of leadership. Where are these leaders leading you? Are they leading you to temporary fame and fortune, to self-righteous gain that will one day wear off? Or are they leading you to eternal life and perspective? There is only one person in this entire universe who can offer eternal life: Jesus Christ. He is the only leader who has ever sacrificed Himself for your life, conquering death by His resurrection. Maybe you haven't accepted Christ yet, and His salvation is new to you. Or maybe it angers you to even read this. I understand. I too was once so filled with pride that any mention of someone else getting the glory made me angry. But God didn't give up on me. He pursued me through His faithful followers. I was blessed to work for individuals who placed Christ first, and by my following them while they served Christ, I witnessed what being a servant really looked like. We often underestimate the impact we can have by serving Jesus and displaying Him at work by instead relegating our Christian life to church activities. But have you ever considered that you may be the only one who shows a colleague what Christ looks like? Maybe someone you work with doesn't know who Jesus is, but they know you. And who are *you* following? If Jesus, then your colleagues should see Jesus through you. Christian leaders show Christ through service and leadership.

Maybe you're reading this book because someone gave it to you as a gift, and you're wondering who this Jesus is. You have never considered yourself a follower of Christ, but you do consider yourself a leader in some form, maybe even a good one. I implore you to continue reading, and I pray that through the Holy Spirit you will be awakened to Jesus as your Savior. Only after that will you find something in this book to make you a better leader.

How Can I Be a Servant Leader?

So, how do we become servant leaders? That answer is not as complicated as it might seem. As we serve Christ, our compassion for others will inevitably change, and our service to Him will carry over into our leadership styles. I've been on the failing end of this endeavor, and it takes constant effort.

Before I really understood what it meant to be a servant, I tried to be a leader. I had good intentions. I cared about others' well-being and helped in whatever ways I could, but I struggled with many other aspects of leadership. I could have taken many different approaches to correcting my leadership struggles, but I tried most of the secular ways with little improvement. I read all the latest books, listened to great leaders tell about their philosophies, and even watched other leaders around me to pick up the latest and greatest way to lead. But none of that worked. Then, I realized I was looking in all the wrong places, and God reminded of this. The first place I should have turned to was the Bible, and when I did, it started to become quite obvious why I was failing: I was not serving Christ as all Christians are commanded to.

As I refocused on serving Christ fully, my whole outlook on leadership changed. Why was I even attempting to lead anyone when I was not being a good follower? As Christians, our main focus should be on glorifying the name of God alone. To do this, we must have our hearts set on Him. Each of us is following or pursuing something or someone. Even the person who works for no one is following a passion or pursuit of something. The Bible calls this act *worship*. Whether you worship yourself, someone else, some physical thing, or even the idea of something, you are worshipping. And if you aren't worshipping God, then you're worshipping an idol in your life. What does this have to do with leadership? Remember that all of us, including us leaders, are following someone. If we are following, pursuing, working toward, or worshipping an idol, then we are not following God. Following anyone other than God is an act of selfishness. Selfishness can never cause a person to become a servant leader.

How we lead will be dictated by our desires. For an example, look no further than the second book of the Bible. In Exodus 32, Moses has been at the top of the mountain receiving the commandments from God. While he was up there, Aaron was in charge of the Israelites below. Moses thought Aaron would care for and lead the people just as God had instructed. However, it didn't take long for the people to become impatient for Moses to return. Aaron could see this, and in an effort to appease them, he instructed them to gather their gold, which he then cast into the fire. From this gold came a golden calf, which the people immediately began to worship instead of the God who had rescued them out of Egypt. Aaron's disobedience to God resulted in his followers straying from their God-honoring ways. Because Aaron was not following God, he led those under him astray.

We humans easily wander when we have nothing to follow. If we don't have a leader, we often create something else in our lives to follow. We've all experienced the temptation to follow idols that promise us some feeling of worth and meaning, but we must resist. God promises us He will help us to do so: "No temptation has overtaken you that is not common to man. God is faithful, and he will not let you be tempted beyond your ability, but with the temptation he will also provide the way of escape, that you may be able to endure it" (1 Cor. 10:13). As leaders, we must not cave in to the fleeting, worldly promises around us, all the while leading both ourselves and those who follow us to death. We must stand firm in the Word of God, pointing others to Christ, the only promise of eternal life. When you zoom out and gain perspective on your leadership, you should realize you're impacting not only yourself, but also those around you. You should see just how serious your responsibilities are.

Aaron took his focus off serving God and instead allowed the people to dictate how he led. He tried serving them by appeasing them. This is the easy way out, and it is not leadership. In doing what the masses want or trying to make everyone else happy by simply granting their wishes, we relinquish our leadership. Remember, the servant aspect of servant leadership is not just serving the people, but serving Christ first and foremost. This is not a call to "perfect" leadership; perfection is impossible. This is a call to follow Christ, and all else will fall into place.

Why Should I Want to Lead This Way?

For Christians, this answer is easy: You should want to lead this way not only because Christ commands us to follow Him, but because the very eternity of someone else may depend on your obedience. Do you find yourself keeping your faith private because you're in the workplace? Do you only lead others to Christ in church-organized events? God hasn't called us to privatized Christianity. Jesus doesn't tell us to "go when you feel like it, and only tell certain people about Me." He commands us to "go therefore and make disciples of *all nations* . . . teaching them to observe all that I have commanded you" (Matt. 28:19–20, emphasis added). This is not a selective command to apply when we feel like it, nor is it a command to a select group of Christians. As followers of Jesus Christ, we are commanded to take the gospel of Jesus to everyone around us. Why would we limit this to church-sanctioned functions? At times, we spend more time at work than we do with family. Therefore, leading others at work includes leading them to Christ. We must faithfully obey Christ in how we lead, praying we display Him in all we do so we can point others to Christ.

If we truly believe Jesus is the only way to eternal life, then why on earth would we keep this good news to ourselves? Charles Spurgeon cuts to the heart of every Christian when he states, "Have you no wish for others to be saved? Then you're not saved yourself, be sure of that!"[2] It should be our utmost desire as leaders and followers of Christ to see those who follow us in turn follow Christ.

If you aren't a Christian, biblical servant leadership is not easy to understand. Before we know Jesus as Savior, we are filled with selfishness and pride that pushes aside any thought of glorifying someone other than ourselves. This is not to say Christians don't also struggle with pride and arrogance—*au contraire*. However, it's difficult to emulate Jesus's leadership style if you don't indeed follow Jesus. You may display certain characteristics of Jesus, but if you aren't attributing your character to the work of Christ, then your actions are a futile attempt to glorify yourself. Think of it this way: you can't hold someone to a standard that they do not believe in or follow. You can't tell someone who isn't in the military to follow regulations that only apply to service members. Why would they adhere to standards they do not submit to? The same is true for someone who does not submit to the authority of Jesus. While you may lead with good intentions and even appear to have Christ-like characteristics, you're just reflecting the common grace God instills in His creation.

Only the Bible can explain clearly why following Jesus is the answer. I can write all day about why you should lead like Jesus and even convince you that this is the best way to lead, but only the Holy Spirit can empower you to understand

2. Charles Spurgeon, *She Was Not Hid* (Metropolitan Tabernacle, 1888).

why serving Christ and leading others to Him is what we were created for. You will not truly understand why anyone would want to lead in this manner until you understand who Jesus is and what He has done for you. If this is you, if you are seeking to understand who Jesus is to you, stop reading this book and pick up the book that points to eternal life: the Bible. Nothing matters more in this life than knowing Christ as your Savior. My prayer for you is that the Holy Spirit would work in your heart right now so that you may know the peace and love Jesus offers. Your salvation means more to me than any leadership teaching I can offer. If you already know and trust Jesus as your Lord, then my prayer is that as we continue this journey together, you will be filled with the Spirit and led to be more like Christ in all you do, especially in how you lead others.

Chapter 2

Value in Serving

The Challenges You Face

When it comes to faith, most Christians tend to be private. Aside from the allotted time throughout the week that we prescribe to be for church activities, many of us would rather go about our days not having to talk about our beliefs.

It should come as no surprise, then, that we feel especially guarded at our places of work. Not only must we face an internal struggle to be open about our faith with people we know little about or with people who don't agree with our beliefs, but we must also face external factors.

In the government sector, there are rules and regulations about religious practices in the workplace. Many of those rules protect religion in general terms, but as with many secular policies, these rules can further particular agendas. What this means is that, while an individual has the right to practice whatever religion they choose within the given rules, someone could still be offended and thus hinder a religious person's ability to practice faith at work. It's the old idea that you can believe whatever you want, just don't tell others about it.

Additionally, while Christians can believe whatever they want in the workplace, many find themselves hindered by how they can actually show their faith. Though many policies in the government sector have been amended to allow more religious freedom, many Christians still find themselves in trouble for displaying, talking about, or reading Christian literature. But can we blame society for hindering our ability to practice our faith at work? Do we turn these hindrances into excuses?

The reality is that no matter what society dictates, we will act upon what is rooted within us. As Christians, do we really believe that Jesus is the Lord of our life? And if so, what could possibly keep us from sharing this with others? I believe the ultimate question we should ask ourselves about our faith and work is this: "Who's really ruling our lives?"

We must understand God has placed us where we are for a specific reason, and we must trust God to use us for His good will. When we obey Him and trust in His will for us, the reward is a joy-filled heart, incomparable to any reward of this world.

We can't share our faith freely until we are walking in God's love and grace. In Philippians 2, Paul reminds the church of God's great love and grace, and he urges them to meditate on this. As the Philippians struggle to grasp the magnitude of who God is, Paul charges them to work out their own salvation in God, pointing out that God's Spirit alone works in them. The Holy Spirit's work is always the will of the Father and always leads to good works. I believe we often misinterpret Romans 8:28 to suggest that God will work all things for "my good" or "what I want." In reality, the good is more along the lines of Jeremiah 29:11, where God reminds us our future in Him is what is good. But when Paul wrote to the Philippians, he was highlighting that we are created to serve God. God is the one who places His will in our hearts, and we should earnestly seek to do His will. When we strive to do His will, God will accomplish His will through us. Knowing that God's will is good is what assures us that our works are not in vain when we're walking with Him. Once we take the selfish blinders off and realize we are not promised earthly prosperity simply because we follow Christ, we can then see the true service in sharing Christ with others, no matter where that may be.

Christians must realize that career work is merely another way to serve Christ. We must stop separating our work lives from our church lives. This separation may be hard to understand since the labors of our jobs result from the curse (referring to the fall of man in which we were cursed to labor the earth). Although it may be true that the curse led to labor, God has still placed us in our specific jobs for a reason. Knowing this, we should seek out the will He has for us in our work lives. Clocking in and clocking out without ever mentioning your faith in Christ is probably not the plan He has for us.

I understand the hardships many government employees face when it comes to sharing their faith at work, and I admit it's much easier to do your work and avoid the religious conversations. However, deep down, we know this is not the will of the Father and the Spirit within us. We were created to glorify God, and this task does not come with stipulations concerning where we work. He has made us in His image so that we may display Him to everyone around us. Even those who don't have a relationship with Christ bear the image of God, but do we see that? Do we believe that? Better, do we treat others like that?

If we have the Spirit within us, and if we believe Jesus is the only way to salvation and eternal life, why do we hesitate to share Him with anyone? More importantly, why don't we

want to share Him with the people we see every day? The
people we work with may not always be our best friends or
the people who help us in times of need, but do they not need
to hear about Christ? We say no every time we don't share
our faith with them. We are saying, "I know you need Jesus,
but I don't have the time to do it right now," or "I am not
the one who should share Jesus with you." We allow many
faulty reasonings to deter us from being faithful and sharing Christ. We put aside the boldness of Christ within us to
ensure a friendship remains, to avoid getting the lecture on
religious talk in the workplace. I am by no means advocating
for you to disregard the rules and policies and get in trouble
or even fired, but I am at the very least asking you to look
within and see who your master is. Are you more concerned
with what a friend or coworker will say to you because you
talk about Jesus, or are you so filled with joy every time you
mention the name of Jesus that no matter where you are or
what you are doing, all you want to do is talk about Christ?
You can be a bold Christian and work in the government
sector. There is such a thing as servant Christians who also
serve their country. Be defined by servanthood of Christ, not
by the workplace in which you serve.

Patriotism and the Christian

One of the most interesting questions someone has asked me
about serving in the government as a Christian was this: "Can
you still be patriotic if you are a Christian in the government?"
To that I boldly say, "Absolutely!"

Just look at the loyalty Moses had to his nation in the
service of God. This was a Hebrew man who was raised in
the Egyptian empire within the royal family and who later
became the leader of the Hebrews during their exodus out

of Egypt. God used Moses, who had a speech impediment, to lead the nation of his people out of slavery and captivity and into freedom under God's command. I would dare say Moses was anything less than patriotic when it came to his nation and the people to whom he belonged. The patriotism that flows within me for my country does not rest in the promises and hopes our leaders give us; instead, it derives from my hope in Christ Jesus as my Lord and Savior and from doing His will wherever He places me. I was born in the United States, so that is where my flag hangs. But that is not where my faith and hope hang.

I have traveled the world, and I've seen many places that do not particularly like the U.S. or allow the open sharing of Christianity. Though I can ensure my "American" doesn't show, I always have a Bible on me, ready to discuss whatever topic the Lord places on my heart with whomever He places in my life. In these cases, my patriotism does not go into hibernation; I just have a deeper sense of doing the will of God. The interesting thing about each one of our nations is that within the boundaries of our lands, the laws that govern us apply only to each respective region. However, the Law of God transcends these boundaries and even more to the different peoples themselves. You see, while we can still be patriotic about our country, this feeling only goes so far and so deep; but the love of Christ within us is unending and has no boundaries.

I'm also frequently asked about the decisions our government makes and how they relate to our faith. Here I remind you that, first, we are to submit to those authorities that are placed by God, and second, that their decisions will be judged accordingly. Unless we are the ones God has placed in an authority position (speaking of higher government), we must pray for those leaders and trust in God's provision as He leads us. In Romans, Paul talks about this type of submission to authority and states that anyone who resists such rule therefore resists "what God has appointed, and those who resist will incur judgment" (Rom. 13:2). I tread lightly here, but it must be said there are times in which a follower can and should speak out against ungodly rule. Even within the government, one does not have to follow such rules and orders that go against ethical and legal decisions. We are not called to blindly follow authority.

God does not, and will not, place us in positions where we must disobey His commandments. We may find ourselves in these situations, but God will always provide us with a way out. Our patriotism or subject to authority will never, and should never, overrule the law God has placed on our hearts. If you find yourself in situations where the decisions you make are going against what God has instituted, then I suggest you reevaluate who or what you are following, because it is not Christ. Knowing the difference between patriotism to country and devotion to Christ will help you know when serving your country becomes more important than serving Christ.

Separate but Equal?

I know you have heard, or even been a part of, the religious debate about separation of religion and work. Most people believe you should not talk about your faith at work, not because they want anyone to have less freedom but because they do not want to hear about religion. There is no problem with *what* you believe in. The issue seems to be *where* you can discuss such beliefs. There is equality in the principle of religion but not so much in the practice of religion. The irony is that most of the people who do not want religion in the workplace still place their faith in something governing their lives: climbing the corporate ladder, cheering for sports, and so forth. People create plenty of time and space to talk about these things within the workplace.

We carve out special time to gather and praise each other for jobs well done, but when someone gives the glory to Christ, the festivities come to a screeching halt. Almost everyone wants to take holidays off, but heaven forbid we actually talk about what those Christian holidays mean. Why can we not mix our faith with our work? I mean, how many people have fancy sayings framed on their desks or walls, sayings which are actually verses or teachings from the Bible, but as long as we remove the reference everything is okay? We wish to surround ourselves with the comforts of Christian beliefs so that they bring "good vibes" to the workplace, but we don't want the ability to openly talk about them.

Whether we openly admit it or even recognize it, Christian teachings are all around the workplace. Flowing within the good order and discipline of the office are the common graces God places in everyone's lives. Whether someone is Christian or not, God bestows common grace to all. This goodness is what makes the world function. It allows "good" people to have success in their lives. Along with common grace, we also see the love of God in the people we work with. Again, whether they may be a follower of Christ or not, God works through people to display His glory. So if these things are already around us, then why do we try so hard to keep them to ourselves or hinder them from discussion? I think one of the even bigger questions is this: If we openly shared our faith in the workplace, how would we affect the whole of the environment?

Think about it: What kind of impact would faith have on the workplace? Would it be negative? If so, in what sense? I mean, just as with any other topic of conversation in society, if someone doesn't wish to be a part of the conversation, they don't have to be. If something is allowed to be discussed, that permission doesn't require participation. I think that is where some of the animosity toward open religion in the workplace comes from. There are some who believe they will be excluded from conversation or that they will somehow be forced to join in. That should not be the case.

What type of positive impact would open discussion have? Aside from being able to talk about what you believe without fear of being shunned or hushed, there are obvious positive implications for Christians who can be bold and share Christ with coworkers. Imagine the encouragement for believers as they grow in sharing their faith with others. From work time to church time—making the two blend together. We bring church to work. We make our work about church.

The funny thing is, there is nothing stopping us from talking about Christ in our workplaces. For most of us, even those of us who work for the government, it is simply in our heads that we shouldn't talk about Jesus while at work. There really is nothing set in stone that says we cannot share Christ at work. Yes, there might be some policies that place boundaries around discussing faith, but all in all, God has already opened the doors for us to tell others about Jesus. The problem is not with the secular rules that govern us. The problem is with our willingness to serve Christ no matter what. Why is it that some who serve the government are so willing to lay down their lives for the good of our country, yet balk at the idea of serving Christ? Quite ironic when you think about what He did for us.

Joyful Service

Along with the struggles of serving Christ in the workplace and the fine line we might draw between patriotism and following Christ, it must be said that the joy in serving Christ, whatever your profession, is the foundation of happiness. As I said earlier, we were created to serve and glorify God in all we do and say, and when we're doing that, true happiness and joy fill our hearts. When you experience this feeling, this overwhelming love of serving Christ, then nothing else matters. You forget where you are or who's around you. All you care about is the warmth of the Spirit in your heart. It drives you to want to serve more. Serving Christ should be our passion. It is this feeling of momentary completeness that sheds light on what eternity with Christ will be like. In this broken world, we experience eternal joy in segments or moments of time, but one day we will have joy unending in the presence of Jesus.

I urge you to serve Christ in whatever you're doing. Share His love with those around you, and more importantly, share His name so that those who do not know Him may have life everlasting.

One of my favorite verses is Colossians 3:17: "And whatever you do, in word or deed, do everything in the name of the Lord Jesus, giving thanks to God the Father through him." This is such a great encouragement for us to serve Jesus in whatever we do. If sharing a meal with a coworker, share Christ! If speaking to someone about our day at work or talking around the breakroom, share Christ! It sounds so easy because it is that easy. The more time you spend with Christ, and the more you read God's Word, the more God will be on your mind and on your tongue.

Trust me, God has equipped you to be the bearer of His good news. Knowing this, along with sharpening your faith in the Word, will bring forth the boldness in you that lies within each and every one of us. Seek opportunities to talk about Jesus. Doing so will strengthen and encourage your walk with Christ. Whether or not you think that what you do and say matters, it does, greatly. The impact we have for God's Kingdom is enormous. The value He places on us is enormous as well. We are either making disciples for Christ or we are working against His Kingdom. As His image bearers, we are created and charged to go into this world, demonstrate God's love, and share Christ. What better place to do this than with the people in our workplace, with whom we spend even more time than our own families. These are the people God has placed in our lives—let's be faithful and share Christ with those around us.

Chapter 3

Leading by Example

The Ultimate Example

People often ask who I think is a great leader or who's had the most influence on my career. For most people, that answer may come quickly—a specific person who either mentored or helped them achieve their goals. For others, it may take some deep thinking, for they may not have had much interaction with a good leader. Some may have had too many good leaders to choose just one. When I answer, I say what many people might find odd, or off-putting, outside of the Christians who know me. For me, Jesus has been, and is, the ultimate example of what a great leader should be. This idea of what a leader should be transcends any organizational boundaries.

Often when we think of a leader, we leave out the part of also being a servant. Servant leadership is not only the cornerstone of this book, but it is the foundation of who Jesus Christ is. In John 13, we see Jesus eating what is famously known as the Last Supper with His disciples. During the meal, after the point in which "the devil had already put it into the heart of Judas Iscariot . . . to betray him" (John 13:2), Jesus rises from the table and begins preparing Himself to wash the feet of His disciples. You can imagine how confused they must have been that their leader, their Lord, was on His knees performing a cleaning ritual, a job usually reserved for the lowest of the low. Jesus then proceeds to tell them,

> You call me Teacher and Lord, and you are right, for so I am. If I then, your Lord and Teacher, have washed your feet, you also ought to wash one another's feet. For I have given you an example, that you also should do just as I have done to you. Truly, truly, I say to you, a servant is not greater than his master, nor is a messenger greater than the one who sent him. If you know these things, blessed are you if you do them.
>
> —John 13:13–17

When we picture a leader, many of us don't include someone washing the feet of their workers. But Jesus did. He humbled Himself in His looming betrayal and death on a cross, all to demonstrate what servanthood is. He even reminded His followers that none is greater than another because of a position. This is the leader we should strive to imitate, one who is serving while leading.

In Ephesians 5, Paul wrote to the church in Ephesus, encouraging them to be like Christ, reminding them to "be imitators of God . . . and walk in love, as Christ loved us and gave himself up for us, as a fragrant offering and sacrifice to God" (vv. 1–2). It's probably safe to say that many of us won't have to give our lives for those we work with, but would you? Does your love for Christ run so deep for others that you're willing to lay your life down in the service of God's Kingdom? I ask this because, as I've said before, it's ironic that many of us will so willingly lay down our lives for a country or an idea, yet as Christians, we hesitate at the notion of laying down our lives in service to God. When we're called to imitate Christ, we cannot leave off bits and pieces of who He is simply because they don't conform to our ideas on how we should serve God. We must follow Christ's example and at the very least be *willing* to lay our lives down in service to Him. This is no easy task—trust me, I know. And by no means am I telling you to purposely place yourself in harm's way to prove a point or to test the waters of your faith. If God desires you to be somewhere that requires this type of service, it will be clear to you. The grand question here is this: "How do we emulate Christ in this manner?"

Emulating Christ's Example

Before we discuss how to imitate Jesus in this manner of servant leadership, we must first grasp our inability to be perfect. We can never match the perfect example Christ gave us. It's easy in our selfish ambition to strive to be better than or as good as the person we're emulating; however, in our fallen and broken world, this isn't possible. Nor can we ever be equal to God.

With that disclaimer out of the way, let's take a look at another of Paul's letters, this time to his dear friend Titus. In the beginning of this letter, Paul gave Titus the qualifications for elders or overseers. Paul writes, "For an overseer, as God's steward, must be above reproach. He must not be arrogant or quick-tempered or a drunkard or violent or greedy for gain, but hospitable, a lover of good, self-controlled, upright, holy, and disciplined" (Titus 1:7–8). This was instruction for picking and assessing elders or overseers in the church; however, I believe this set of guidelines is equally applicable to those who also oversee any of God's children in any capacity. If we are to be the Church, representing God in all aspects of our lives, why then would we not hold ourselves to the same standards? As leaders overseeing others, we are to emulate these characteristics of Christ. Notice the selection of words used to demonstrate this kind of leadership. None suggest that we must present ourselves as worthy of any position, but rather as humble servants to those we serve. This humility is a direct reflection of our relationship with Christ, and the character traits listed in Titus 1:7–8 stem from following Christ.

Practically speaking, though, how do those characteristics look in our workplace? For the leader who is also a servant, they manifest in someone who earnestly seeks the good of those under the leader's influence. This earnestness is not always easy to accomplish. If you focus too much on certain individuals over others, you are showing partiality in your decisions. However, making decisions in light of what's best for others shows you care, and when others know you care, they will see something different in you. This is what a Christian leader should strive for, to be noticed as "different." Being different can lead to conversations about what makes you different, thus giving you the opportunity to talk about Christ.

Another way this leader is set apart from the crowd is by being upright. Again, uprightness flows from one's relationship with Christ, and it ties directly to faith in what Christ has done. To be upright is to be planted firmly in something, to have a solid foundation. Not only will this display confidence in the decisions you make, but when others know you're firmly planted in Christ, they will trust the decisions you make. If leaders practice these characteristics, they won't be overcome by greed or arrogance. As children of God, nothing can overcome us.

We have a firm foundation because the Holy Spirit resides inside Christians and establishes their relationship with God.

Once we are in the hand of God, nothing in this world can remove us from His grip. We are firmly rooted in Christ, and we can rely on His protection over us. Jesus tells us,

> I give them eternal life, and they will never perish, and no one will snatch them out of my hand. My Father, who has given them to me, is greater than all, and no one is able to snatch them from out of the Father's hand.
>
> —John 10:28–29

If being in the grip of God is not reassuring, then I don't know what is! This assurance gives us power to serve Christ in all we do!

We also have a firm foundation in God's Word. Through the Bible, we literally have the Word of God in our hands. We should turn to it every single day, feeding on the words and teachings of God. Among the great books to learn from, the one book that matters most is often set aside in favor of self-help books. If you stopped reading this book right now and picked up the Bible instead, that would make me the happiest author ever. Reading the Word of God every day is vital to knowing who God is and what He expects of you. All other books, though there are many important ones, are secondary.

But there is another way we learn and grow in God, and it's our third foundation in Christ: prayer. Prayer is how we fellowship with God, having the great opportunity to come before the Father, thank Him for all He has done and is doing for us, and ask of Him whatever we desire. We often overlook or put aside prayer because it's not comfortable to do. For some reason, we think that we have to speak eloquently to God or that we don't know how to speak to God, but

Romans 8:26 reminds us, "Likewise the Spirit helps us in our weakness. For we do not know what to pray for as we ought, but the Spirit himself intercedes for us with groanings too deep for words." We must stop relying on ourselves and realize that everything, by the power of the Holy Spirit, is the work of Christ.

Be the Light in This Dark World

It's not easy being a Christian now, nor has it ever been. Paul told Timothy that "all who desire to live a godly life in Christ Jesus *will* be persecuted" (2 Tim. 3:12, emphasis added). Jesus also reminds us that if we wish to follow and serve Him, we will be treated as He was treated. Need I remind you that He was mocked, ridiculed, beaten, and eventually crucified? Does this sound like a good life for Christians? I'm not quite sure if this was left out of your initial understanding of the gospel, but it is precisely the life you will live as a follower of Christ. Now, one person's struggles may be vastly different from another's, but in any case, simply labeling yourself as a Christian does not promise an easy life by any stretch of the imagination. However, amid this challenging yet rewarding path, we are called to be the light of Christ to those around us. For Christians in leadership positions, this means displaying Christ in our daily routines and decisions. From the way we speak to others to the way we carry ourselves—it all matters. You may not see the direct impact of emulating Christ, but I promise, you are sowing the seeds of His Kingdom. Keep planting the seeds of the gospel, and God will water them.

One of the hardest struggles for leaders is believing that we're doing good things for others, though we may not see or feel it. Humans feed off gratification—we need some sort of physical understanding that what we do matters. Yet we must cast this need aside and trust that what God has us doing will bear fruit at some point. We need to understand that not everyone gets to see the seed turn into fruit from start to finish. Paul reminded of this when he wrote, "I planted, Apollos watered, but God gave growth. So neither he who plants nor he who waters is anything, but only God who gives growth" (1 Cor. 3:6–7). As faithful followers of Christ, we are called to be the light and share the gospel, and God will do the rest. This concept goes hand in hand with the Titus 1 principle: A good leader cannot be greedy or arrogant. Nothing we are doing should be for our gain, but all for the glory of God. By being the light, we are radiating the glory of Christ in us, portraying Him in all things. Being a light to this world should not be confused with being *in* the spotlight. We must shine the light of Christ *on* others. Think of holding a flashlight when it's dark. We do not walk around with it pointed on ourselves; we point it outward to light up the darkness around us. The beauty of being the light of Christ for others is that this light comes from within us, radiating through us from the Spirit. He knows we desire to be a part of this work; therefore, He shares His joy by using us as His hands and feet.

Leading Others to Christ

Being a light through leadership draws others to Christ. Being a leader is an awesome calling. I don't mean *calling* in the sense that only certain people should do it, but rather that it's an opportunity God gives you to serve Him. A leader is someone given much responsibility, usually over other people's lives. How you execute your leadership matters. When it comes to emulating Christ in leadership, the purpose is not to make yourself look better or to advance yourself up the company ladder. For the Christian leader, emulating Christ and displaying the light of the gospel to those around you leads others to Christ. As I said earlier, our whole purpose is to bring glory to God in all we do—that is why we were created. As image bearers of God, we are to lead others to the cross and the work of Christ. This is the whole point of why we are to be like Christ in our leadership style.

This might seem like an obvious point, and I wish it were so obvious to all of my brothers and sisters: In the hustle and bustle of life and in our efforts to be the best at what we do, evangelism is often ignored. For some reason, leaders trade comfortable offices and corporate high-fives for their opportunity to let Christ shine through them. This is contrary to God's commands. He commands us to glorify Him, and that means sharing Christ and leading people to Him, making more disciples. Let me put it quite frankly. If you find yourself seeking to serve God yet stopping short of sharing Christ or pointing to Christ in your leadership, you are not bringing glory to God. I know it is uncomfortable to be told that what you are doing is wrong or even more that what you are doing is disobedient. But I ask you, what would you label it as?

There are two simple explanations if you find yourself in this predicament. Either you desire your image more than that of Christ's, or you do not fully trust in what Christ has done for you. The former is a direct impact of the sin inherent in each of us, namely pride, which is the root of much of the sin in our lives. We know what is right and what is commanded of us, yet we fulfill the desires of the flesh more because they often give us instant, yet fleeting, satisfaction. We want to serve Christ, but when we should point all glory to Him, we instead divert that attention to ourselves in some desperate attempt to make ourselves look better. This is just as bad as doing nothing at all! We are aimlessly trying to steal God's glory, and I can assure that such attempts will not work. We've manipulated the gospel so that it fits our lives, making us unfaithful. Manipulating the gospel to fit our own desires reveals that we are not truly following Christ.

We might lean on the crutch of being a "new believer" or claim some other excuse for not sharing the gospel. There are many other reasons we might fall short of emulating Christ or pointing to Christ in our leadership, but if we find ourselves in this state, we ought to take a good hard look at whom we are serving.

The encouragement in all of this is that salvation is the work of Christ alone, by the Spirit alone. While we may fail at times, there is nothing we do that can derail the work of God. If you read through that last paragraph or two and thought to yourself, "Man, this sounds like me," don't be discouraged. I too have been there. Jump into the Word, repent, and ask God to use you in serving His Kingdom. Remember that God uses broken vessels to carry His gospel to others. Imagine a beautifully crafted wooden box. Unfortunately, it has holes all around it. It won't hold much in it. But seemingly useless wooden boxes are exactly what God uses to spread His love. He uses us in our broken state, pouring into us so that He can pour out through us. Imagine such a wooden box filled with water. With all the holes, the water will pour out all over the place.

There is no comparing to the love God has for us. While we may look at ourselves and recognize that we're not serving God as we are commanded, there is still hope. We are still in the positions and places God has placed us in to serve Him. Call on the Lord to forgive you of your sins, and commit to following Jesus as your Lord and Savior for the rest of your life. Ask the Lord to use you. Be faithful in sharing Christ and pointing those around you to Him and His work of the cross. Share this love for Jesus with those around you. Dwell on the rich grace and mercy God has had on us, and go out and make disciples for Christ!

Chapter 4

The Meaning of Work

I remember my first job working at a Dollar Tree stocking shelves and cleaning. It was not the ideal work for a young teenager who'd rather have a job with more recognition, especially when the minimum wage at the time hovered around five dollars. Nonetheless, that job showed me what it meant to work hard for something and how to enter the workforce from the ground level. I learned how to manage time in order to efficiently get the job done and how to place items on a shelf to look professional and draw customers' attention. Looking back, I really appreciate that job for what it gave me, but I missed out on one very important aspect that I recognize only now: the *purpose* of my work. Of course, there was purpose *to* my work: I was working hard so I could make money. But the purpose *of* my work was lacking.

The substitution of these two simple words may seem trivial, but they are the foundation to the meaning of our work. To understand where I'm coming from, let's first take a look back at Genesis when God instituted work. After God created the world and everything in it, He then created man, Adam. God then placed Adam in the Garden of Eden, a beautiful place full of every kind of plant and animal all living in harmony, so that Adam could work there and care for it, glorifying God in his work (Gen. 2:15). Adam enjoyed work, honoring God with it, and there was no pain in his work. But in Genesis 3, Adam and his new partner, Eve, disobeyed God and ate from the forbidden tree. Their punishment was banishment from the Garden of Eden, and even more, separation from God. After their removal from the Garden of Eden, the world became full of sin and death. The animals no longer lived peacefully together, and the plants that once provided nourishment had to be tended continually. The work Adam and Eve now faced was a punishment for their sins. But let's not miss the beauty in this story. God did not banish them and leave them forever. He set the stage for redemption and a future glory through His son, Jesus. The work man now finds himself doing is not meaningless, for we still glorify God in it. But now work is twofold: First, we work tiresomely because of the fall of man, and we also work to serve Christ and point others to Him.

Your Job as "Work"

This concept of work as punishment is not something we easily appreciate, especially since many people feel it's not "fair" we are still paying for the sins of the first man. Here, we get hung up and miss out on the foundational point of work, which is to glorify God. Before we go any further, let's clear up the point that work in and of itself is not punishment. It was established before sin entered the world. The aspect of punishment is seen in the toil and unending hardship involved. It's easy to see how work glorifies God and builds His Kingdom when one serves in a church or ministry, but what about the rest of us laypeople? How do we common workers use our job as God-honoring work?

The first step is to stop thinking about our jobs as something bad, something we must do to survive. We must change the way we view work. I get it: Not every job is fun or desirable. But if it's where you are, you must honor God in it. If we work every day solely clocking in and out to get a paycheck, we're missing the people and purposes God has placed in our lives. If you stop right now and think about how many people in your workplace do not know Jesus, and how many times you have talked to them about Jesus, how do you feel? Do you feel as if you are being obedient to God?

The purpose *to* your work may be boring. Your job may be something you never imagined yourself doing, but it's the only job you can get right now. Or maybe it is the most exciting thing you get to do all week; you're at your dream job and living life. But the purpose *of* your work is what fills you with joy when you wake up in the morning, knowing today is the day you get to share and show Christ. There is a vast difference between being *happy* with what you do and being *joyful* in what you do. When we serve Christ in our jobs, our work turns to glorifying God, and that is what we were made for. That is what will satisfy our souls. Sounds easy enough, right? So, what does this look like in your job?

Serving God in the workplace starts with love. First John explains the love of God and how to love our neighbors. To show love, we must set aside our selfish desires, choosing rather to seek and do the will of God. When someone is struggling with a project that's approaching its deadline, we can help them accomplish it for their good instead of sitting by and watching them fail so that it makes us look better. Offer to take a coworker to lunch; you'll be surprised how this leads to sharing Christ. (Well, you shouldn't be—Jesus loved sharing meals with strangers and sinners!) Simply taking the time to talk to some people is enough to brighten their day. The point is to seek opportunities to share Christ. God sought us when we were sinners, so in like fashion, we should follow His example and seek those who do not know Him.

The Challenge of "Work"

The challenges many of us face when it comes to serving Christ in our jobs are the many rules that restrict talking about religion in the workplace. This is especially so in the government sector. At times, the restrictions can feel so daunting that the thought of talking to someone about Jesus at work is scary. Is potentially losing your job worth it? This is a tough question to answer. I have wrestled with it many times before, and the answer I keep coming to is similar to missions. We should not look for trouble for gratification or self-satisfaction, but we also should not run from trouble—specifically the chance to speak the name of Jesus. The difference between the two mindsets is grace. One person is "hunting" for fights on religion; the other seeks grace in his approach. If you find yourself attacking others more than listening to them, God is not behind your work—some selfish desire is. If love is not present, God is not present. On the other hand, when an opportunity to talk about Christ presents itself at work, we should not cower from it or stay silent for the sake of comfort. When a coworker has a legitimate question about God, don't change the topic or brush it off. Stand firm in your faith in Christ and share the gospel.

Sharing our faith at work is not easy, I get it. I mean, for the most part, people don't even want to share their faith with their closest friends, let alone people they work with. Add to it the fact that much of our identity is rooted in our jobs. Yet this brings up another heart-wrenching question: Is your identity in your job or in Christ? As you read this, you know deep down that identity should be rooted in Christ, but how many of us can say our lives demonstrate that? I know I struggle with that all too often. We spend more time at work throughout the week than we do reading our Bibles or sharing the gospel. And therein lies the problem. If you put all of your time for a week in a spreadsheet, I could almost guarantee the "God column" would be on the low end. This is not a finger-pointing contest. I am right there with you. Even as I write this, my heart sinks because I know I should be spending more time with God, and in turn spending more time serving Him in my job. What are we going to do about it? Are we just going to continue on in our ways, or are we going to act in faithful obedience to God? Even if you feel like you have it together, spend more time with God, serve God more, and take a brother or sister in Christ along with you.

Missions "Work"

I don't know about you, but I absolutely love missions work. Serving Christ around the world fills me with such joy! There's nothing like looking into the eyes of a young child who has never heard the name of Jesus. As you offer her food and tell her of Jesus's love for her, you can see the Spirit flicker in her eyes. Displaying God's love in the mission field is not reserved for overseas arenas or in inner city missions alone. The mission field is all around us on a daily basis, including our workplaces. When you realize that your place of employment is a mission field, your perspective of work will change. You will see the purpose *of* your work.

When I realized my job was a mission field, my whole perspective on work changed. I saw opportunities to serve God like never before. As I mentioned earlier, my passion is in the overseas mission field, and one of the great things about my job is that I get to travel all over the world, essentially for free! When God removed my sinful blinders, I was awakened to the fact that God had placed me in a place of work that would allow me to travel the world and take His gospel to those I meet. I can't describe the joy I found in knowing my work was set up to honor and glorify God. I had worked for years without serving God in the way I was meant to; therefore, when I understood the purpose *of* my work, I began to love what I did in ways I never imagined. As odd as it sounds, I felt like a missionary who was employed by the government!

What is your passion in serving God? Is it missions? Is it creating things or serving people food? Whatever it is, find that passion and determine how God has placed you in the position to serve Him fully. Your job is a mission field, and the sooner you see that, the sooner you can see how God wants you to serve Him. The beauty in serving Christ is that there are no boundaries to the manner in which we serve, or to the people whom we serve. The Great Commission in Matthew tells us to "go" and take the gospel to "all" peoples. This means that whatever and wherever our work is, there are people who need to hear about Jesus, and we are to share Jesus with them! It's so exciting to write about this because I can share in your joy as you realize the opportunities your job has for you to share Christ. I remember when the Spirit enlightened me: Oh the excitement I had when I came to know the purpose *of* my work!

I pray that you too will find this purpose and seek to serve Christ in your job, and if you are already seeking this, I pray you will take brothers and sisters along with you and that God will provide you opportunities to serve Him in your work and glorify His name through you. If you don't see how your job is glorifying God, spend time in the Word and in prayer. Don't try to figure it out on your own. Trust me: That does not work. You will only find selfish avenues to quench your desires. If you truly wish to honor and glorify God, you need God in the equation.

Chapter 5

The Ultimate Sacrifice

What comes to mind when you hear the word *sacrifice*? Is it the Old Testament picture of an animal on an altar, killed to appease God? Is it the image we see in *The Hunger Games* when one individual takes the place of another to possibly die? Is it making time for someone in our busy lives or giving to another in need? For some of us, this word brings jarring memories of friends and loved ones who have laid down their lives in the service of our country. One of my favorite verses to reflect on is John 15:13: "Greater love has no one than this, that someone lay down his life for his friends." Whatever your picture of sacrifice, at its most basic level, it is giving something up for another. Sacrifice takes us out of our comfort zone to provide something to someone else. Whether food, water, money, time, or life—sacrifice takes something from us and gives it to another person.

Where does ability for physical or emotional sacrifice come from? It comes from God, our loving Father, who since before creation planned to sacrifice His only Son, Jesus, in order to restore our relationship with Him. The cross is the ultimate picture of sacrifice. Of course, there are other pictures throughout the Bible which depict sacrifices, some foreshadowing the ultimate sacrifice in the New Testament;

but no sacrifice will ever be comparable to what Jesus did for us on the cross. Most of us won't be called to physically lay down our lives for someone, but this sacrificial love that Jesus teaches and displays is something that is within us, whether we recognize it or not.

The sacrifice on the cross shows us a love that only God can provide and a sacrifice that required a physical death to free us from sin. There may be a time when you must lay down your life for another, but more often than not, the sacrifices God calls us to are daily. Jesus has already provided the ultimate sacrifice for us, and with that we have life in Him. How comforting and encouraging it is to know that! We should not allow fear to control how we serve Jesus. Our lives should constantly worship and glorify God in everything we do. So what does daily sacrifice look like?

Why Lay Down My Life for Someone Else?

Countless saints have laid down their lives to advance the gospel and bring us the Word of God. The early church experienced this kind of sacrifice on a regular basis. In this case, each individual did not make a sacrifice to benefit themselves, but to advance the church. Let's take a look at Stephen, one of the first martyrs in the New Testament. His death was not intended for a particular person, but rather for the church at large. Not only did his death glorify God in that he was faithful to his last breath, but it provided a picture of faithful service to those who would follow in his missional footsteps. Through the sacrifices of the early martyrs, we see the church exploding in growth and emboldening future missionaries to go and share the gospel with the world.

Every year, my wife and I go to Nicaragua to share the gospel with some of the most wonderful people I have ever met, and every year I pray for protection for our team. I know in the back of my mind we are heading into the unknown, and quite honestly that drives me crazy. But I also know that God has called us to go and share His gospel, and if that requires me to lay down my life, then so shall it be. This last year, Nicaragua experienced internal strife that bordered on yet another civil war. With this news came some tough decisions for our team. We decided it was best not to go for safety reasons. This was one of the hardest decisions I've ever made because I love those people, and even more because I've always felt called to be a missionary regardless of the dangers. Through much prayer, we came to this decision because there was more than just my life at stake. There was an entire team of people who depended on our decision-making to keep them safe. While I believe on a personal level that dangerous places will not hinder me from sharing the gospel, I also believe that God has instilled discernment within us through His Holy Spirit to guide others and keep them away from danger. I wholeheartedly believe that if God calls us to serve in the most dangerous places, we are to serve faithfully. However, God does not call us to live in a manner that places us in danger for the sake of thrill. Seeking danger outside the prayerful consideration of what God has planned for you is only self-satisfying and prideful.

Aside from seeing sacrifice in martyrs and missionaries, we can also see it in everyday death. When followers of Christ lay down their lives for their country or friend with the Spirit driving their love, this sacrifice honors and glorifies God. We don't always have the scripted death we see in the movies in which our last words are the perfect quote for our tombstone, so our lives must speak for us. If we love Jesus, and live for Him, it should be apparent in our daily lives. If it is apparent to those we interact with that we love Jesus, then our death in sacrifice for another will demonstrate our love. When our fellow service member who loves Jesus dies in the line of duty, we will not say, "He did it for the love of his country." Instead we will say, "He did it because he loved Jesus." Even in war, death can be a testimony to the love of Jesus within us. This is what we should strive for: not to be the next headline martyr in a mission field, but to be the next follower of Christ who glorifies God even in the most common death.

Jesus Is the Ultimate Sacrifice

If you are a follower of Christ, then you know that Jesus is the ultimate sacrifice. His sacrifice is the cornerstone of our faith. But if this idea seems foreign to you, I invite you to read Hebrews 10:1–18. This need for a sacrifice did not develop as sin continued to plague the world—instead, God had always planned to redeem His people and fulfill their need for a Savior. In order to accomplish this redemption and satisfy the wrath of God which was rightly intended for us, God sent His only Son, Jesus, to live among us and be the sacrifice that would bring us back to God. In the Old Testament, we see redemption foreshadowed with the sacrifice of animals, namely the lamb. In the New Testament, Jesus became the sacrifice, and His blood covered our sins. Because He is the ultimate sacrificial lamb, we no longer need animal sacrifices to appease God. Jesus's death not only atoned for our sins, but also demonstrated the love of God for us. This is the love we are called to emulate to everyone so they too can see God in us.

The sacrifice of Jesus on the cross was so powerful to those who followed Him that when it came time for many of them to be put to death for being His disciples, they chose other means to die than on a cross. If you study Roman history, you'll know that death on a cross was by far the worst form of punishment. It was painful and gruesome, and no one has ever survived it. But their choosing otherwise was not because they were afraid of this form of death; it was because they believed they were unworthy to die in the same way as their Savior. Peter, one of Jesus's closest followers, could not escape the punishment of the cross, so he chose to be hung upside down. Think about this for a second: Jesus's sacrifice was so empowering for His followers that they were willing to die for His name's sake. Not only this, but they did not even count themselves worthy enough to die in like manner as their Lord. What has changed since the early church that makes Christians now flinch at the idea of laying down their lives for the church? Again, I'm not advocating placing yourselves in harm's way, but I am questioning our trust in the power of Jesus. While we may not be called to die for another in the name of Jesus, at the very least we should be ready to.

Have No Fear to Serve Jesus
One of the biggest factors that hinders us in serving Christ to our death is that we have grown distant from Him. Why would we want to lay down our lives in the service of someone we are not familiar with or have little faith in? Remember earlier when I said that our main purpose in life is to worship and glorify God in everything we do? One way we do this is by living our lives like Christ did, by emulating His life. To be like Christ and live like Him, we must know Him and be close to Him. Think about this: When you stand close to a mirror, you have a pretty clear picture of your reflection. The farther you stand from the mirror, the less you can see yourself clearly. You will always have an understanding of

what you're looking at; however, you will forget the intricacies and details you saw when you were so close and focused. Take a rearview mirror for instance. When a car is on your tail, you can see the person driving fairly clearly. Maybe that person is on the phone, eating, or putting on makeup. Yet, when the car drifts off into the distance behind you, you still know someone is in the driver's seat because at one point you saw someone driving. You may no longer know what they are doing, but you know what they were doing.

The same holds true for us as we strive to live for and like Christ. When we are close to Him, spending time in prayer and in the Word, we are familiar with what God is doing in our lives and what He desires for us. When we distance ourselves by not spending time with God, we lose sight of what He's doing in our lives and forget the promises He has made to us.

It's quite comical the amount of time we invest in things we care about, like music for example. We can hear a song a few times, and boom, it's stuck in our heads forever. However, we can spend hours in the Scriptures, and the moment we stop reading and studying, we immediately start forgetting what we've read. This knowledge should drive us to spend more time in the Word, not less. But for some reason, it doesn't. We let the fear of failure drive a wedge between us and God. Like most things, we believe we have some control over our lives, and failure actually scares us because we know what it feels like. I encourage you to let go of even the smallest aspect of your lives. I know it's a scary thought to not be in control, but the more we try to hold the reins, the more we let pride and fear get in the way of faithfully following Jesus.

In the previous section, we talked about Jesus being the ultimate sacrifice and how His death mended the broken relationship we had with God. But that's not the end of the story. The most beautiful and powerful part of that story is the resurrection of Jesus from the dead, overcoming and conquering death so that we as Christians could live and reign with Jesus forever. If that doesn't get you excited about following Jesus, I'm not sure what will! Knowing that Jesus died for you out of pure love and then rose from the dead to overcome death for you is the power of the gospel. Our mighty Lord and Savior has triumphed over death! What power we have within us through the Holy Spirit!

Live Sacrificially

To have power over something is to be truly free. Christ has conquered death and reigns at the right hand of the Father (Eph. 1:20–23). With the Holy Spirit in us, we share in the power of Christ to live for Him. Often, when Christians hear the term "live sacrificially," they immediately consider how to spend less money and give more. Maybe you think of all the things you have around your home and how you can give some of it away, really only making room for more stuff. When you think about it, how many seasons of sacrifice have you gone through? How many times have you felt convicted to change the way you spend or to downsize your life, only to refill the closets or fall back into unguarded spending habits? For me, this seems like a never-ending cycle. I find myself truly enveloped by the power of Christ and make changes in my life to live more sacrificially; then in the blink of an eye, I'm putting less in the offering plate and spending more on worldly things.

The reason many of us continue to go through these seasons is that we're not sacrificing what means the most to people and what is pivotal to the mission of reaching the lost:

time. Now, I in no way intend to overlook the value in sacrificing money (which we are called to do); I'm simply suggesting
that as with most parts of our lives, we are only giving up
what *we* either do not desire or find the easiest. What's easier
and more convenient to sacrifice, the twenty-dollar bill you
drop in the offering plate without even thinking or the hours
investing into someone who does not know Christ? Honestly,
we become so attuned to dropping money in the offering
plate that it doesn't even hurt anymore. Does that sound
sacrificial to you? If we aren't constantly in prayerful consideration and reflection on the monetary blessings God has
bestowed upon us, then we will not give accordingly. We all
go through ups and downs with income. Simply giving what
you've always given is not the sacrificial offering required of
Christians. When God blesses you more financially, yes that
money may allow you to go on a vacation or get something
nice for your husband or wife, but it also allows you to give
more to the Kingdom. If you're reading this and feeling upset
or uncomfortable, you should. But I can promise you that the
more you faithfully give to the Kingdom of God, the more
joy you will find in your heart.

So, what is missing and what is needed to live more
sacrificially? As I stated earlier, Christians must invest their
time in people. This is twofold. First, we must invest time in
our brothers and sisters in Christ so that we can sharpen and
encourage each other; second, we desperately need to invest
time in those who do not know Jesus as their Savior. Time is
one of the hardest commodities to sacrifice because we have
only so many of those precious seconds each day. Whether
we're working, going to school, raising a family, or just trying
to find time for ourselves, we are constantly dividing our time
according to what's important to us—yes, *important* to us. I

understand that work and our families, even our quiet time, are important, and I am not encouraging you to cut back on those things. Quite the opposite. I am asking that you use these times in your life to live for Christ. In my opinion, work is one of the greatest mission fields we are given. For most of us, we see our coworkers as much as, if not more than, our families. We are literally given the time to invest in these people around us, yet many of us overlook or outright ignore the opportunities to share Christ.

There is physically no way to make more time. What can be done, however, is for you to use the time God has already given you and the environments God has already placed you in. When Jesus traveled from town to town, He met the people where they were. He didn't add time to the day in order to accomplish more; He used the ordained time from God to reach the lost. Jesus didn't complain there wasn't enough time in the day; He rose early in the morning to spend time with the Father in prayer and then went out to the lost. While we don't know much about the life of Jesus when He was a young child and carpenter, I imagine He lived and worked a life that reflected the love of God. I don't for one second believe that He ministered to the lost in the stories of the Gospels only. I know that during His whole life He lived and worked for His Father God. We are to do the same. As Christians, we must work diligently in whatever avenue God has placed us for the Kingdom, living like Christ and using this time with others to share the gospel.

This seems like an easy concept, right? Go to work, which we already do, and share Jesus. However, for many Christians who work in different government positions, this is not as easy as it sounds. There are some limitations when it comes to faith in the workplace. So how do we use the time at work to share Christ? Well, for starters, *live* like Christ. Most often those around us *see* what we believe before they hear it. And if your life is reflecting Jesus, it will be very obvious that something is different about you, and that will draw people to ask what it is that makes you different. If you work in a place that hinders you from sharing your faith, one of the best ways to overcome this restriction is to have others engage you in conversation first. Do you know how to accomplish this? You got it: Live like Christ! It's hard for someone to get upset about you sharing your faith when they were the one who asked about it. Remember, the Holy Spirit within us does the work, and the Spirit draws others to us. If someone is curious about Jesus, then the Holy Spirit is working in them. No one genuinely wants to know about Jesus without first being regenerated. I often like to picture the Holy Spirit within me connecting to the Holy Spirit working within that person, and the power behind that picture is beautiful.

I pray this for each and every one of you reading this:

Father, thank You for loving me even when I am unfaithful and disobedient. Thank You for the sacrificial love You have for us and for displaying that love on the cross, and for sacrificing Your only Son to redeem and restore us to You. Jesus, thank You for taking on the wrath that was meant for me, and for conquering death so that I may have life in the Spirit. I pray that You will open our eyes to the people You have placed around us who need to hear Your name. Give us the strength, courage, and wisdom to speak Your gospel in their lives so that they too may receive eternal life with You. Remove the fear that binds us and shine through our lives as we seek to live for You. As we go into our places of work, may we enter into the mission field which You have called each of us to with the love, hope, joy, and peace You give us. Shine through our lives, Lord, so that others may see You and not us. Use our ransomed lives for Your Kingdom. Forgive us where we fall short. We love You, Lord, we praise You, Lord. We glorify You and You alone. Thank You for pursuing us when we did not deserve it. Use us now to pursue those You have called. Amen.

Chapter 6

The Armor of God

Like most young boys, when I was a kid, I often imagined I was either a cop or a soldier, constantly ready for the bad guys to attack. Being ready required maintaining the upper hand, and having the upper hand meant having some form of weapon. To find such gear, I often raided my stepfather's duffle bag for his military gear. As with any boy of my time, I usually had a good toy gun ready at all times, but some of my favorite items to wear were my stepfather's camouflage helmet and Kevlar vest. I remember these specifically because at my house, there is still a photo of me wearing all of my gear with camo paint on my face, standing in front of some bushes (yes, you can still see me). Growing up in a military family, combat and defensive gear shaped my vision of what armor should look like. It protects us from pending dangers. As I've grown in my understanding of the Bible, I now see the spiritual connection of armor as we defend our faith and share the gospel.

When you hear the word *armor*, what picture comes to mind? Do you imagine a modern warfare soldier outfitted with the most cutting-edge gear? Do you imagine your own military gear? What about the early centurion—the Roman soldier who was dressed in the most prestigious armor of the times? Even if you've never been in the military or law enforcement, movies and television shows give us a picture of what armor is. Generally, armor is used to protect our most vital body parts. In this chapter, we will talk about the armor of God in Ephesians and how to use it in our daily battles.

Imagine you're the leader of a group of soldiers preparing for battle. You and your troops are getting ready to stand against the toughest army ever faced. There is no option to back down, and your soldiers trust you as their leader. You all know what lies ahead, and you're ready to fight. Knowing that war means possible death, wouldn't you want to make sure your soldiers have the best armor available? Of course you would, and so does God. He has provided the best armor for His followers. He knows what lies ahead, and better yet, He knows the outcome already (spoiler: He wins).

What Armor Do You Have?

When Paul was writing to the Ephesians, Roman centurions were some of the most lethal warriors, and the Roman Empire was flourishing because of its strong army. These soldiers were outfitted with the most stunning armor. Before the battle even began, they would send a clear message to their enemies: "We do not back down." As Paul wrote this letter to the church in Ephesus, he used the image of the Roman soldier's armor to prepare Christians for the spiritual battles awaiting them. He urged the church to find strength in the Lord, reminding them and us that our strength comes from Jesus alone. Interestingly, this war is not against flesh and blood but against darkness and spiritual forces. Many of you may know exactly what I'm talking about, for you struggle with the battles weighing on you right now. My prayer is that you will heed Paul's call and put on this spiritual armor.

Picture a Roman soldier standing at the ready, a beautiful and rugged golden helmet with red horsehair standing tall on the top, a cast iron breastplate engraved with the outline of muscles to intimidate the enemy, his handcrafted leather belt to hold his uniform in place as he fights, shoes with spikes on the bottom for holding firm his position. In one hand, he holds a magnificent shield that bears the crest of his kingdom and in the other, he holds his kingly sword made specifically for him. This is what you look like donning the armor of God. You wear the helmet of salvation as a crown to let all others know you belong to God's army, the breastplate of righteousness to proudly boast the work of Christ, the belt of truth to hold you firmly in the promises of God, shoes that allow you to stand firm in your faith and to take the gospel of Jesus to all nations, the shield of faith that extinguishes the flaming arrows from the evil one, and the sword of the Spirit—the living Word of God. This is the Christian: a beautiful yet rugged warrior of God.

When we read through Ephesians 6 and see this armor from God, it should excite us as leaders. Jesus reminds us through Paul's letter that we will face trials and struggles, but there is good news. Not only is Jesus by our side, but we are outfitted with the armor of God to fight for the Kingdom we will inherit. Oh, and by the way, Jesus has already conquered Satan and the evil forces for us! As a leader, this knowledge should encourage you to live for Christ and take the challenges that surround you head on. It should also empower you to ensure your brothers and sisters in Christ are wearing their armor. What is it to be the only soldier in the army wearing armor to a battle? Yeah, you might last a little longer, but everyone around you will fail. Remember when we talked about being in a spiritual war? Well, we are fighting this war together. At times, you may feel isolated, as if you're fighting alone, but you are not.

As a leader, you need to know your people. You should be able to recognize when someone is fighting a battle so that you don't bark commands when someone may not be in the best physical or emotional state. What that person may need most is for you to share in the fight, not add to it. One of my favorite depictions of a good leader is a comic that circulates on Facebook every now and then. The first picture shows a person sitting atop a throne, above everyone else, yelling out commands while the people below push and pull to move the leader around. The next picture shows a person on the same level as everyone else, standing in front stating, "Follow me!" I love this because that second person is leading and fighting with the people around him. That is the battle we fight with Jesus as our leader. He's right there with us.

There are two reasons people don't use their armor. The first is that Christians know they have access to it, but they think either they're not entitled to it or that they don't need it. The second is that they use some but not all of it, and the neglect renders them vulnerable. Imagine again a soldier ready for battle but not wearing his breastplate, helmet, shield, or worse yet his sword. This underprepared soldier would be ineffective and vulnerable to an attack. The same holds true for us Christians and our spiritual armor. If you aren't wearing the belt of truth, you won't fall back on the promises of God when a battle arises; you'll lean on some worldly comfort and find yourself losing the fight. If you aren't using your shield of faith, you'll find yourself easily succumbing to temptations or wavering when something challenges your faith. What if you're out sharing the gospel, but you aren't wielding your sword of the Spirit? You may find yourself talking less about Jesus and more about yourself because you are not using the Word of God. I urge you to use all your spiritual armor. Don't think for one moment that you can face the battle with anything less. We cannot fight this spiritual warfare on our own.

How Do You Use This Spiritual Armor?

Paul says simply to put it on, but how do we don something spiritual? First, we must pray. Paul reminds us that praying at all times is the foundation to our perseverance. If we use our armor improperly or without God's help, it will not work. There is a purpose to our armor. Not only is it for our protection against the evil that surrounds us, but it is also for spreading the gospel of Jesus. Both require God's help. This may sound foreign to you, for often it seems as though we are in a defensive position or constantly under attack, leaving little room to be on the offensive. However, we are commanded to take the gospel to all nations, and doing so does not come easily, hence the reason God has given us such armor.

Each individual piece of armor has a specific purpose that allows us to persevere. The helmet of salvation is a daily reminder that we are saved by the blood of Jesus and that we belong to Him forever. Nothing can pluck us from the hand of God (John 10:28–30). This encouragement fuels us as we prepare to fight the negative thoughts the devil attacks us with. Our minds are easily distracted, and they often welcome many tempting thoughts which lead us astray. Knowing this, we must prepare daily for the battles that lie ahead by turning to the Word of God and renewing our minds in His promises for us.

The breastplate of righteousness not only bears witness to the glories of Christ, but also guides us as we strive to be like Him and display His glories to those around us. It reminds us that we are living for Christ and not ourselves, that there is nothing righteous within ourselves but rather, it is the righteousness of Christ that grants us salvation. Just as the helmet guards our minds, the breastplate guards our hearts. When unprotected, the mind and heart become dangerously susceptible to temptation. Culture tells us, "Follow your heart," but Jeremiah 17:9 and Matthew 15:19 tell us the opposite. Instead, we must trust in Christ and follow Him. These are the desires Psalm 37:4 describes.

The belt of truth is the foundation to our faith. Jesus tells us He is the way and *the* truth, not *a* truth. Jesus is the foundation and cornerstone of what we believe, and resting in these truths gives us peace (Matt. 7:24–27). Knowing there is truth in what you believe gives you freedom, and being able to reflect on God's promises provides us the strength we need to face the battles ahead. An interesting point about the belt is that this one piece of armor held together all of the attire and provided a firm housing for the sword. If the belt was loose, the gear would fall or the sword would not come out in time when the soldier was fighting. We put little emphasis on a belt, but it holds everything together, just as truth holds our faith together.

The shoes allow us to stand firm in our faith and ready us to take the gospel to the world. Think about the spikes in the bottom of the Roman soldiers' shoes. These spikes allowed them to hold steady when they stood together to form a wall, making it very difficult for the enemy to move them. The same goes for you. When you dig in as the world pushes against you, you will be able to stand firm in the faith you have in Jesus. The shoes also allow you to take the gospel to the nations (Rom. 10:15). Think of these shoes like track shoes, which also have spikes. Having a firm footing is vital to standing firm!

Then comes the shield of faith, which is our protection from the temptations Satan throws at us. I love Paul's imagery here when he describes the shield which "extinguishes the arrows." Such arrows are the daily attacks Satan tries to distract us with. Not only does our shield protect us from getting hit with the arrows, but it puts the flames out as well. This shield is what allows us to stand unwavering in our faith when we approach battles. Knowing we are protected from the flaming arrows is a sign of our trust in God, our faith on display for others to see. While a shield is typically a defensive tool, it can also be an offensive tool to the enemy who sees us standing in our faith as we're attacked. Think of the psychological effect this has on others, especially an enemy. It's tiring to attack someone to no avail.

When the time is right, you can wield your final weapon—your sword. The sword of the Spirit, which is the Word of God, is the gospel at work. The sword is the truly offensive aspect of our armor; it slays the falsehoods that surround us and cuts deeply into the souls that deny Christ. It is the Spirit alone who turns the heart to God, and this turning comes when we faithfully spread the Word of God to those who don't yet have salvation in Christ (Gal. 4:6). Our sword both defends us and conquers the world. However, we must not viciously attack others. We must walk in the Spirit and graciously share Christ with those around us. Remember, this sword is of the Spirit, not of us. Therefore, we are conquerors in Christ and not in the world. Our work should be done to further the Kingdom of God and bring glory to His name.

We fail when we go to war without our armor, and we must put on *all* of our armor. We must be in constant prayer for both ourselves and our brothers and sisters alongside us. This is especially important for you as a leader. Remind your brothers and sisters to put on their armor, and be in prayer for them. All too often we spend time praying for the battles we face yet forget to pray for the battles our brothers and sisters are facing. If you are a leader and find yourself surrounded by what feels like the enemy, put on your armor and pray as you prepare to fight for them. Remember, this armor is also meant to spread the gospel to those around you. It protects you as you face the challenge of sharing the Truth with people who are avidly against hearing it. It strengthens you when you feel as if there is nothing more you can do. It holds you together when you feel the world closing in on you. It upholds you as the enemy unleashes everything they have to push you down. Stand firm.

Stand Firm in Your Faith

One of the most beautiful pictures of heaven to me is that of Jesus sitting at the right hand of the Father. The peace illustrated in this completeness gives us the earnest desire to be with our God. Jesus is sitting because He has already destroyed the enemy. He has won the war. There is so much comfort in knowing we cannot disrupt God's plans, especially when we know He works out His will for our good and ultimately His glory. Here on earth, however, we still have battles to face; therefore, Paul urges us to stand firm. We are called to stand because we still have work to do. God is still sanctifying us, and sanctification comes with trials that draw us nearer to Him and sharpen our faith. To do this, we must be standing, ready to take on the battles that lie ahead. The hope throughout our struggles is that while we still have work to be done in us, Jesus is with us every step of the way, indwelling us with the Holy Spirit. He does not leave us alone to fight.

What makes standing firm so difficult? If you have a weak foundation, you will be easily moved. Your underlying belief or understanding of who God is may be faulty. Remember when we talked about having a solid foundation in who Jesus is? Your faith stems from trust and confidence in Him. If you believe Jesus is *not* who He says He is, or if you cannot understand His Word, then you don't have a solid foundation to stand firm upon. When someone challenges your faith, and you turn to a faulty belief in Christ, you will be shaken. Does this sound familiar? Have you ever found yourself at work or with friends, and the ever-elusive topic of religion actually comes up in conversation, but you either shy away or silently pray no one asks you about your faith? Maybe this feeling results from your foundational beliefs. Ask God for understanding, and He will guide you (James 1:5). Most of us experience faulty foundations at some or many points in our walk with Christ. These experiences led Paul to tell us to "work out your own salvation with fear and trembling" and to seek discernment as we grow closer to Christ (Phil. 2:12). We must have a firm foundation to stand upon.

As a leader, you will have people look up to you in ways you may not even realize. When the organization starts to shake, they will turn to you for guidance. If you are not firm in your stance, then your followers too will begin to shake. If they know you are following Christ, though they may not follow Him, they may turn to you in times of struggle. They may come to you with challenges at work or even personal issues. Don't miss the chance to let Christ shine. If you don't have a firm standing in your faith, then you won't point them to Jesus. You will end up giving them some good secular advice or maybe a watered-down version of who Jesus is, but you won't share what Christ commands you to share: His gospel.

The workplace is one of the hardest areas in which to stand firm in your faith. Working for the government puts you in even more of a hard place. Aside from the policies and restrictions, there is this stigma about government workplaces and religion, as if they are oil and water that can never mix. We place chains on ourselves in our faith, whether we scare ourselves out of talking about Christ because we fear what may happen, or we avoid talking about it because we don't want to upset the leadership ladder. But we must stand firm in our faith and be ready to share Jesus at any moment. Psalm 116:16 is a beautiful reminder: "Truly I am your servant, LORD . . . you have freed me from my chains" (NIV).

As a leader and follower of Christ, you must stand firm in your faith. You have been placed in leadership for the work of the Kingdom, not for your glory. We must remind ourselves of that fact daily to succeed. It's so easy to slip into the mindset of "me first" or "for my glory." We idolize ourselves as leaders because we want to be seen and recognized. Don't allow your foundation to crack. Stand firm in Jesus and what He has done for you. You are a leader for Christ, so lead people *to* Christ.

Battle Gracefully

The battle call rings out, "Stand firm." We must prepare for such battles. Put on your armor, defend where needed, and attack (take the gospel) as well. This is where I caution you. As warriors, sometimes we swing the Sword of the Spirit too eagerly, without regard. I urge you to battle gracefully as you serve the Lord. Paul gives Timothy some advice we all should heed: "And the Lord's servant must not be quarrelsome but kind to everyone, able to teach, patiently enduring evil, correcting his opponents with gentleness" (2 Tim. 2:24–25). Picking fights with believers and unbelievers is not showing the love of Christ. Being quarrelsome, argumentative, confrontational, or combative is not the way to teach anyone about Christ. Paul reminds us to be patient and kind, which applies to both brothers and sisters and those still unbelieving.

We all have brothers and sisters in Christ with strong opinions about certain topics, whether the topic is scriptural or secular. And we have our own opinions about these topics. Can you think of a time when a fellow believer started discussing an opinion, and because you didn't agree, you became frustrated and lashed out? I have found myself in this situation, lacking grace and allowing pride to rule. It's OK to have discussions with fellow believers you don't agree with, but how we conduct ourselves in this moment is what reveals the heart. I admit, I have been less than kind at times when I'm "defending" my faith. This reaction is wrong and forsakes the very grace God shows us. If, like me, you feel yourself becoming combative, step back and ask God to give you the patience you need for the conversation. Or, in love and kindness, you may have to walk away from it altogether. Remember, Christ showed us love when we did not deserve it, so we too must demonstrate love in the way we "fight" for Christ.

Another challenge for Christians is how we "battle" our enemies. It's easy for leaders to separate themselves from their enemies or completely destroy them. Of course, for most, it is much easier and less combative to just distance themselves from those they disagree with, but some do find joy in annihilating their opponent. But are these loving responses?

Take a look at Romans 12:9–21, which is titled, "Marks of the True Christian":

> Let love be genuine. Abhor what is evil; hold fast to what is good. Love one another with brotherly affection. Outdo one another in showing honor. Do not be slothful in zeal, be fervent in spirit, serve the Lord. Rejoice in hope, be patient in tribulation, be constant in prayer. Contribute to the needs of the saints and seek to show hospitality. Bless those who persecute you; bless and do not curse them. Rejoice with those who rejoice, weep with those who weep. Live in harmony with one another. Do not be haughty, but associate with the lowly. Never be wise in your own sight. Repay no one evil for evil, but give thought to do what is honorable in the sight of all. If possible, so far as it depends on you, live peaceably with all. Beloved, never avenge yourselves, but leave it to the wrath of God, for it is written, "Vengeance is mine, I will repay, says the Lord." To the contrary, "if your enemy is hungry, feed him; if he is thirsty, give him something to drink; for by so doing you will heap burning coals on his head." Do not be overcome by evil, but overcome evil with good.

This passage highlights love and tells us how to "fight" the enemy. We must be hospitable and patient with those who need to know who Jesus is. This is so hard for us, though, because we don't like opening up to others, especially those we don't know well. We are also impatient. So how do we overcome these feelings? By being in constant prayer and meditating on the Word of God. These two acts will reveal not only God's commands to us, but also His will for us.

This week, as you step back into your leadership role at work, reflect on this passage and strive to display these marks of a Christian. Pray that God will give you opportunities to hold fast to what is good and to stand firm in your faith. Show hospitality to someone who does not know Jesus. Show your coworkers you are not haughty and full of yourself, but full of the Holy Spirit. If you find yourself toe-to-toe with an aggressive unbeliever, remember the armor of God that you bear, and rejoice in the hope that Jesus gives us, patiently enduring the trials before you. Do not take it upon yourself to repay the evil you feel was done to you, remembering that the Lord will repay evildoers. Feed your enemies the Word of God and lead them to drink of the living water providing them eternal life, so that they never thirst again (John 4:14).

Chapter 7

Service before Self

Throughout our lives, we are presented with values which, if important to us, we cling to and make a part of our entire being. In the Air Force, one of the core values is "service before self." Even before I ever considered joining the military, this idea of sacrificial service was instilled in me by my family. The servant nature we feel within us comes from being image bearers of God. When we are selfish and push aside our desire to help or serve others, we act in complete disobedience to our Creator. Often, if we knowingly ignore a cry for help or pass a homeless person on the corner, we feel a stirring inside, a knowledge that we should have helped. Yet we rationalize ourselves out of helping by thinking, "Someone else will help that person," or, "They will spend the money on something like alcohol," all the while suppressing the deep sense that we should help and serve that person. That feeling welling up inside us is a call to action from the Holy Spirit.

As Christian leaders, we make decisions that reflect either the Holy Spirit or our sinful flesh. Could someone look at our leadership style and know we truly care about our people, or do we treat those who work for us like that homeless person on the corner, rationalizing ourselves out of helping? This is the crossroad many leaders find themselves at early in their leadership career. Do you take the path that leads straight to the top, climbing on the backs of those around you? Or do you take care of people, all the while missing out on a few opportunities? There is a misconception that we must choose to be either a ladder climber or a people person. Fortunately, many recent leadership books encourage relationships. In other words, you can be a successful leader and still take care of the people you work with. It all starts with how you serve others.

Service vs. Self

Let's come back to that crossroad where we must decide how to conduct ourselves as leaders. If you've already experienced this crossroad before but feel you need to be a better leader and follower of Christ, it's OK to circle back around to this pivotal decision point. As you stand at this intersection of choosing to serve others or self, think about why you are in the position you are in. If you immediately envision your successes or your image, then you can guarantee you are serving self. If, however, you reflect on the fact that God has placed you where you are for a specific reason, to glorify His name and point others to Christ, then you are ready to serve others. We must cast aside the desires of the flesh and put on the righteousness of Christ in order to serve others. Remember what it costs us to follow Jesus: everything. He tells us to leave the things of this world behind if we are to follow Him. He provides everything we need to serve others.

If we desire to serve and help others, why then when the time comes is it so hard for us to do? Well, put simply, we battle pride. Pride is the root of much sin in our lives, and it is no different here. In some form or another, we believe we can bring something to the table. Instead of letting Jesus shine through us and our actions, we either suppress His light and go about our business, or we manipulate our service to reflect ourselves instead of Jesus. By doing this, we put ourselves before Jesus so that we receive the praise. This pride also falsely leads us to believe we are filling some void in others' lives, rather than Jesus filling that void through us. Most often, we don't make these claims outright, and we may even feel offended at such an idea, but what do our actions say? Do you find more joy when someone praises you for your service, or do you find joy when you get nothing while Jesus gets all the praise and glory? I know this is tough to swallow—I am right there with you. We are surrounded by a sinful culture that tells us, "me first."

The beauty of the gospel is that Jesus will always be glorified. Just as there is nothing we can do to make the story any sweeter, there is also nothing we can do to derail the story or take from its sweetness. As a leader, you should find great peace in knowing that even if you've failed in the past in how you treated people or how you selfishly attempted to serve others, God was glorified. This knowledge should also shape how we serve others as leaders from this point forward. At the forefront of our minds should be the truth that we were made to glorify God. He put us in positions to serve Him first, and our service to others should point to Jesus, bringing glory to God's name. Our pride constantly tries to influence our decisions; feeding on the Word and promises of God is the only way to overcome these thoughts. If you, like me, find yourself struggling to serve others, pray that God will imprint your purpose and His will on your mind and heart so that you can serve Him and those you lead.

Our Leadership Shaped

If you already consider yourself a leader, someone or something at some level has likely impacted the way you lead. It may be a family member, someone you worked for or with, a mentor, or a book. Our outside influences shape us, whether we realize it or not. I've been fortunate to know and learn from many great leaders who have impacted the way I view leadership, but there are a few bad leaders who have shaped my leadership style as well. We tend to emulate good leaders by walking and talking as they do, and from bad leaders we tend to learn what not to do. For the bad leaders, note what not to do and how not to act. We know what it feels like to work for an unfair or even abusive boss. It leaves a mark on us so that we don't want to treat others wrongly. When we encounter a leader, we take notes on their style. Why do we not do the same with Jesus?

Encountering Jesus for the first time changes our lives. We are made into new creatures, changed from the inside out. Why then do we leave His teachings at church or at home rather than bring them with us into the workplace as we lead others? We talked earlier about the leadership examples that Jesus has given us and that we are created in His image; but for some reason, that truth doesn't always translate into our leadership at work. Not only do we have the greatest example of what a good leader is, but we have the everlasting Word of God to show us—it's given to us in text! We see the pride problem and God's answer, yet we selfishly disobey. We lose sight of our purpose to serve and glorify God, and therefore look to worldly solutions. Remember, there is nothing we can do to alter the will God has for us. Call out to God to write His will on your heart and make His desires your desires.

Pray that He will use you in your leadership to point others to Christ. He will answer.

Most of the things we've talked about are not new concepts. My desire is to point back to Christ in our leadership styles. I know many great brothers and sisters in Christ who are also great leaders, but to what measure? To the praise of those around them? Or to the awards and accolades that line their office walls? This is me at times, and maybe this is you, too. Therefore, our measuring stick, our standard, should be that of the life and teachings of Jesus. He is who we claim to follow, and He is the one we should emulate in our leadership. We talk about how we are moldable by outside influences, yet in our flesh, we seek other people to shape us. My wholehearted desire is that you do not see me in any of this, but that you see and seek Christ alone. Pray that God will shape your mind and heart to be able to serve Him and to lead others to Christ, not just to better careers. The Bible must be our go-to book for advice, and Jesus must be the first person we seek to emulate. "Do not be conformed to this world, but be transformed by the renewal of your mind, that by testing you may discern what is the will of God, what is good and acceptable and perfect" (Rom. 12:2).

Our Leadership Projected

Our leadership development is not a one-way street. As we are influenced by others, so we influence those working with us. Ideally, good leaders are making more good leaders. In order to do this, we either inadvertently influence people, or purposefully teach others how to lead. We unknowingly impact those around us. We go about our day as usual, without the slightest thought about how we lead and influence others. How many times do you stop before making a decision and think, "How is this going to impact and mold others around me?" Typically, we make the decision and move on to the next, thinking more about how this will impact the company or workplace. I know it is impractical to say we must stop before every decision and determine how our leadership is affecting those around us in terms of molding new leaders, but we should spend time mentoring others in how and why we made certain decisions, especially impactful ones.

To continue the cycle of building good leaders, we must invest time in those with leadership potential. This isn't to say we neglect the others or pick and choose our successors. However, there are people who stand out as future leaders, and spending quality time teaching them will not only contribute to their success, but it could save them from making the same mistakes you have. As I mentioned, we often unknowingly project our leadership style on others, mainly because we forget others are watching, but we should pay attention to who's watching. There must be purpose to our teaching others, just as there is purpose to our leadership. If we don't spend time shaping and mentoring future leaders, we're leaving them to their own understanding.

Imagine you are in school, sitting in the classroom, and the teacher walks in and says, "Welcome, now read the entire book, and you should be good for this course." You probably panic because this is all new material to you, and you have no idea what's important or what will be on the test. You don't even know what to study! This is no fun. We like and often need to be taught what is vital to our learning and what we should focus on. If you don't mentor others, they will feel like the student in this poorly constructed class.

Aside from serving God and others through leadership, shaping and teaching new leaders should be a top priority.

When Paul was traveling, he was teaching followers of Christ while also mentoring new teachers. He could have traveled around to teach followers and not concerned himself with mentoring others. Of course, we see the issue with this already: At some point, the teachers would be no more. But that is not God's plan. God placed Timothy in Paul's life so he could learn how to be a future teacher. How did Timothy learn from Paul? He penned letters to the churches, he traveled and passed messages which are now books of the Bible, and he heeded Paul's advice. This is the model for leading and teaching. If you know someone who would be a great leader one day, allow that person to see some behind-the-scenes decision-making, and even ask their opinions. Start shaping that person to lead as well as follow.

The most important aspect of mentoring is reflecting Christ in our teachings. Just as we have talked about earlier, God has placed us in these positions to impact the Kingdom, not just the company. If we teach others to be better versions of ourselves, we're not teaching them how to be more like Christ. You may have been a leader for a long time and only recently realized your impact in the workplace. Maybe mentoring someone to be the next leader is what you were placed there for. And what better way to disciple others than to teach them about Christ! It's OK to give Jesus credit for your success as you teach others. Remember, it's not about our praise, but the praise of God. It's so joyous to be able to point back to Christ when someone asks you how you deal with a situation or how you make decisions at work. Be purposeful when you teach.

What Does Selfless Leadership Look Like?

When I was a young leader, my troops and I had a high visibility exercise which was being evaluated by one of our top leaders. We spent days out in the field, constantly dealing with different scenarios. It was long and exhausting, and at the end, the commander stood in front of everyone and applauded me on my leadership and what I had done. I remember looking out into the faces of those with me and seeing and feeling what being exalted over others feels like. It was a horrible feeling. They had been the ones standing watch throughout the nights. They had been the ones executing the decisions that not even I alone had been making. Yet, for some reason, I was the one getting credit. Unfortunately, recognition in this manner is seen often in the military or government sector. This is not what selfless leadership looks like, and I learned very quickly that it does not feel good to take the credit for others' work. That moment early in my career taught me a lot about what it means to take care of those around you. From that point forward, I was determined to serve others while leading.

Selfless leadership is giving credit to those who deserve it, to those who actually carry out your decisions. Selfless leadership is working a shift for someone when they need family time. It is choosing to make decisions for the good of the people and not solely for the good of yourself, your career, or your organization. It's also taking the blame for failures that result from your decisions. Selfless leadership should hurt sometimes. As leaders, we should feel the pains of those around us. Leadership is sacrifice. As Christians, we look to Jesus for an example of sacrificial leadership. He is our teacher, our leader, our Savior. Not only does Jesus show us the way to lead others, but He also shows us what ultimate sacrifice is. Jesus literally laid down His life for His followers so that they could have life abundantly and forever in Him. In the military, we hear many stories of sacrifice. Sacrifice is putting John 3:15 to work. The sacrifices we have seen by those who serve with us are heart-wrenching and move many others to service. But even these sacrifices pale in comparison to what Jesus did for us. In Him, we have everlasting life. As leaders, are we making sacrifices to glorify ourselves, or are we making sacrifices that point to the cross of Jesus and what was done for us? Is our selflessness purposeful?

"I give thanks to you, O Lord my God, with my whole heart, and I will glorify your name forever" (Ps. 86:12).

Chapter 8

Serving God and Country

To serve God and country—what a powerful and moving thought. This phrase is filled with nobility and has been yelled on battlefields for centuries. When I hear this, I picture an army preparing to fight for a throne or homeland, lined up with swords in hand, awaiting the uplifting message from their commander to charge into battle. I imagine William Wallace, riding his horse up and down the sea of troops, rallying with the closing words, "For God and country!" While this may be the picturesque setting for serving God and country, it's not quite what happens in our daily lives. The service I want to talk about here happens more in our daily work, specifically in the government positions we may hold. What does it mean to serve God and country? Even more so, what does it look like to serve God while serving our nation?

What Is the Difference?

For some, this may be an easy question to answer. Of course serving God looks like following Jesus and obeying His commands, pointing to Him in all we do. And of course serving country looks like serving in the military or in any position that supports the government. These are very much elementary answers, but they shed light on the fact that many people draw a distinct line between serving God and serving country. To add to the distinction, our nation's history appealed to God in its foundation, imposing language throughout our founding documents which point to a Creator. Most of us walk around with these reminders in our pockets, with the words "In God We Trust" on the money we cling so tightly to. Yet, when asked whether religion was meshed with the foundation of our nation, many will outright deny the idea. Others will find creative excuses to downplay the Founding Fathers' intentions. Deep within, we want to acknowledge God as the Creator, but the pride of our nation swells up to draw the line which attempts to separate God and country.

Thankfully, no amount of pride can actually separate what God has created and intended. As followers of Christ who also serve our country, we should dwell on the psalmist's words in Psalm 33 and daily remind ourselves that we are a nation created for God—not a nation marked by earthly boundaries or cultural seclusion, but a nation God made for Himself. This word *nation* confuses us so often because we have blurred the understanding between people and territory. When the psalmist writes, "Blessed is the nation whose God is the Lord, the people whom he has chosen as his heritage" (Ps. 33:12), he is talking about the Israelites—not the land, but the people born of the promise to *Israel*. In the New Testament, Jesus comes to transcend the people group lines and graft into the vine all people God has chosen.

When we look back at the Jewish culture in the Old and New Testaments, we can see pride in who they were. Similarly, we see much pride in being Americans. Both groups feel "chosen," either to rule the holy land or the world. With each of these, it seems the underlying issue is submission to authority, namely the authority of God. For centuries, the

Jewish culture was called to submit to the authority of God, and while the Bible shows many accounts of the Israelites' wavering faith, the biggest issue within the people's hearts was submission to Jesus as Savior and Lord. For Americans, the irony lies within our rebellion against the throne of England, which we no longer wanted to submit to, founding our own country filled with rules which many don't want or follow. There is an underlying rebellion to authority that lies within each of us. Therefore, in Romans 13, Paul reminds us to "be subject to the governing authorities" (v. 1) and that "rulers are not a terror to good conduct, but to bad" (v. 3). Since the fall, man has never wished to blend the ultimate rule of God with the limited rule of man. While there are periods of obedience, something within each of us challenges the authority of God and wants to replace His law with our own.

Take our justice system, for example. Though there are glimpses of commandment language in many of the laws, there are more misguided interpretations by man littered among them. We often fear reprimand from the world before that of the Creator. How often do we skip to thinking about the punishment from society, only later to realize how it offends God? Let's use a clearly man-instituted law as an example: speeding. We are much more fearful of getting pulled over and having to pay a fine or having bad marks on our license or insurance than we are of how this offense may affect our testimony as Christians. Have you ever found yourself speeding, cutting people off, or driving less than safe because you had somewhere to be, as if your time is more important than someone else's? And of course, what happens later? You and that other person pull into the same parking lot or same place. What if you were on the way to church or to work where you've been sharing the gospel with that person? How do you think this would affect your ability to lovingly share the gospel with that person?

As followers of Christ, we must stop trying to separate what it looks like to serve God and also serve our country. There is only a difference because man has made one. God never intended there to be a distinction between serving Him and serving the country we live in. We must quit trying to appease society and the culture around us and start focusing on worshipping and glorifying God in service to our country. While serving our country, we are to be serving God, pointing others to Him in our work and service. Matthew 8:5–13 provides a beautiful depiction of this service. While Jesus was in Capernaum, a Roman centurion came to Jesus and pleaded for Christ to heal his paralyzed servant. This is amazing. A Roman centurion (who, by the way, worked for the government that would later crucify Jesus), who had the power and authority to command armies, approached Jesus and asked Him to heal his servant. Jesus told him, "I will come and heal him" (v. 7). We see a Roman soldier with authority, but Jesus saw the centurion's heart. The centurion said, "Lord, I am not worthy to have you come under my roof, but only say the word, and my servant will be healed" (v. 8). Jesus replied, "Truly, I tell you, with no one in Israel have I found such faith" (v. 10). Because of the centurion's faith in Jesus's authority, his servant was healed.

Do we have faith like this? Are we willing to set aside the authority we have on earth to submit to the authority of Jesus? This Roman centurion was serving a government that openly denied Jesus's authority and hung Him on a cross, yet he believed in what Jesus could do and was not ashamed of it. This Roman, who had much power, displayed a great act of submission to authority by openly approaching Jesus to ask for help. Many of us profess Christ and serve a government that at the very least allows our profession of faith, yet we try to separate the two. We willingly submit to governing authorities; however, we shyly submit to Jesus, who is our Lord. We are proud to fly our American flags or post patriotic statuses on social media, yet we cower at the opportunity to serve Jesus while serving our country. I challenge you to stop separating your faith from your service to your country. There are so many bold Christians who do just this. Will you be one of them?

Stories of Service

One of the most rewarding aspects of serving this country is getting to meet those who've paved the way in their service and sacrifice to our nation. I've had the opportunity to meet living heroes that most only get to read about or see on television. Even more encouraging is getting to know them and their faith in Jesus as Lord and Savior. What amazed me most when I spoke with or got to know many of them is that there was no line between serving God and serving the country. It was as if they knew their mission was to serve God while they served the nation they called home. Admittedly, they had their fair share of challenges and even borderline discrimination, but they chose to cling to Jesus and what He means to them. Their boldness in Christ not only compelled me in my writing, but it also challenged me to be the leader God called me to be and to persevere in all aspects of my walk.

See, one thing we tend to forget is that leaders are rarely, if ever, placed in a position of leadership at the beginning of their career. More often than not, and especially in government service, one tends to start at the lowest levels of followership. Even if you are placed in what seems to be a leadership position somewhere in the middle of the order, remember, you are still following someone.

I've been blessed to have encountered some amazing, godly leaders in my career thus far on all ends of the leadership chain—from someone who defied many odds and challenges to climb to the highest ranks in the enlisted core, to someone who is still climbing high in the general officer ranks. These leaders have taught me that no matter what culture tells us or what policy tries to enforce, Jesus Christ is the most important person to follow. One of the most important things I have learned from a dear friend and brother in Christ, Chief Master Sergeant Rick Parsons, is that investing and devoting time in others is what the gospel of Jesus is all about. I look back at the time he devoted to my spiritual well-being and can see the intentionality of the gospel rooted in our time together. Whether it was taking time to eat lunch with me and talk about the Bible or allowing me to tag along at golf outings where we talked about different biblical topics, Rick invested time in me to show me what a bold Christian leader should be.

Another amazing leader I recently served with overseas was Brigadier General Kenneth Ekman. Rarely does someone get the honor of working directly for a general, especially at my level, and even more rare is a leader who is a bold and outspoken Christian. General Ekman exemplified what it means to lead people with passion, and it was clear that his passion for others came from his love for Christ. I have never met someone who was so dedicated to actually knowing the people he worked with, and he never forgot anything about them.

I remember one day specifically. I was just returning from an extended journey in our host country, and I was in the dining area completely exhausted and waiting to chow down on a salad (you tend to crave things you cannot have). General Ekman came in, saw me, and sat down to eat with me. I expected this to be more of a "how is the mission going" brief, but it was far from that. He did ask how I was doing, but then he asked about my family, whom he knew by name, and how school was going. His knowing that I was in seminary led us to deeper theological conversations since he too was a Christian. I was amazed at his openness about his beliefs. I had presumed that leaders at that level shielded their beliefs in an effort to avoid confrontation or to play the political game. Not General Ekman. He told me, just as Rick did, that God placed him in this position to lead for Jesus and show others what the love of Jesus looked like. This idea of using work as a platform to share Jesus has sunk into me deeply. Service to God and others shouldn't come only when it's convenient; it should result on purpose to point to the greatest leader in history, Jesus Christ.

The Greatest Story

When you read a great book, someone tells you an amazing story, or you see a movie that changes your life, what do you do? Do you go hide and keep this great news to yourself? Or can you not help but tell everyone what you now know? This is the gospel within us, the greatest story ever told. As Christians, we have the Holy Spirit living in us; we have the gospel imprinted on our hearts. Yet, for some reason, we keep it to ourselves, or even worse, we only share it with select people. This love that comes from Christ is not a selective love. Quite frankly, Jesus loves us just as we are. There is nothing we can do to earn it, and there is certainly nothing we can do to lose it. Why are we keeping this great news to ourselves? Jesus came down from heaven to dwell with us and show us what a loving and caring leader looks like. Not only this, but He then willingly died on the cross as the sacrifice for our sins so that we could be reconciled to God. Our Savior showed us what true love looks like, and then He acted out that love by redeeming us so that we could live with Him eternally in heaven.

The greatest story of leadership, service, and sacrifice lives within us. Whether you call yourself a leader, or whether you think you are serving this country, you are called to share the gospel of Jesus in whatever capacity you may find yourself. Don't try to hide the flame within you. Be the guiding lamp for someone to find Jesus. You don't have to be a general or CEO to be the ultimate leader in someone's eyes. You just have to be faithful and obedient to share the gospel and point others to Christ. You never know if you are sharing Jesus with the next Paul.

Conclusion

If there is one thing you get from this book, I pray you know that Jesus is your Lord and Savior. Being a good leader pales in comparison to being a follower of Christ. I don't expect you to finish this book and become the world's greatest leader, but I do expect you to finish this book and want to know more—not more about how you can become a better leader, but more about how you can become a better follower of Jesus.

For those who started this book already following Jesus, I pray that you will be moved to glorify God in your workplace, that you will dive into your Bible and seek to reflect Christ in all you do. Writing this book has given me the opportunity to address many shortfalls in my leadership. There is not one of us who is perfect. If you read this and felt as if nothing applied to you, I hope it at least stirs you to spend time in prayer and ask God to show you what needs to be addressed. Our work matters. Our service to our country matters, even beyond the sacrifices we make. Someone around you needs to hear the gospel. Take up your armor and prepare for battle, because I guarantee that it is around you, whether you recognize it or not. God has equipped you to stand firm and boast in Christ. Remember, the challenges we face and the suffering we may endure is meant to draw us closer to God. Rely on Him and trust in His promises. Ask God to reveal someone to you at your workplace to share the gospel with, and ask for the boldness and courage to speak the truth of Jesus in their lives. You have the light of Jesus within you, so be the light in this dark world. We are made in the image of God and are to imitate Him. We are exactly where He wants us to serve Him. We *can* serve both God and country.

Acknowledgments

It is my honor to acknowledge the following people in their support of this book:

Ariel Waiters

Charles Martindale

Dan Jones

Danny Hammond

Deb Root-Aguilar and Ruben
    Aguilar

Donna Holcomb

Francis Luk

James Bunyard

John Wayne Lambert

Josh and Angie Rodriguez

Kalyn Wilson Photography

Kevin Root

Kim Johnson

Larry McEntire

Lee Andrews

Luke Blackwell

Michael Voto

Nisha Cheeseman

Ronald J. Eldridge

Ruth Lovejoy

Samantha Burrill Westman

Shane Tatum

Truth Ministries

Wayne and Lee McCallister

THE KINGDOM ADVANCEMENT PROJECT
HIS KINGDOM | OUR PASSION

At the Kingdom Advancement Project (KAP), our passion is the mission God has called each and every one of us to do—share the Word of Jesus Christ. We began by serving Christ in the mission fields of Nicaragua and felt a void of the physical Word of God, the Bible, in the areas we served. It does no good to build up groups of people around the idea of God, without having the foundation of His Word. With this, KAP began and since has placed an emphasis on getting Bibles to people around the world.

- We currently serve churches and missionaries in Nicaragua, Pakistan, and India.
- Every $5 provides a Bible to someone who needs to hear the words of Jesus.
- To date, we have provided over 400 Bibles to people in these countries!
- **All the proceeds from this book will go to KAP to continue to serve around the world.**

Please visit our website www.theKAP.org to see our work and view projects that may require special donations. Please continue to pray for those we support as many are in areas that do not allow the open preaching of Jesus or Christianity.

"Therefore go and make disciples of all nations, baptizing them in the name of the Father and of the Son and of the Holy Spirit, and teaching them to obey everything I have commanded you."

—Matt. 28:19–20a (NIV)

About the Author

Mike Root is an officer in the United States Air Force, an entrepreneur, and a writer. He began serving his country on active duty shortly after college and has deployed to several countries, including Jordan and Pakistan. Shortly after entering the armed forces, he started his first business, Troy Transit, which offered safe rides to students and residents. Mike holds two master's degrees, the most recent in Theological Studies from Liberty University, and is currently a PhD candidate in Public Policy at Liberty University. He and his wife, Michelle, co-founded The Kingdom Advancement Project, which provides Bibles and resources to missionaries in Nicaragua, Pakistan, and India. All of the proceeds from this book will go to support this charity (www.theKAP.org).